MOTORCYCLES
I'VE LOVED

MOTORCYCLES I'VE LOVED

Lily Brooks-Dalton

RIVERHEAD BOOKS
a member of Penguin Group (USA)
New York
2015

RIVERHEAD BOOKS
Published by the Penguin Group
Penguin Group (USA) LLC
375 Hudson Street
New York, New York 10014

USA • Canada • UK • Ireland • Australia
New Zealand • India • South Africa • China

penguin.com
A Penguin Random House Company

Library of Congress Cataloging-in-Publication Data

Brooks-Dalton, Lily.
Motorcycles I've loved / Lily Brooks-Dalton.
p.   cm.
ISBN 978-1-59463-321-8
1. Brooks-Dalton, Lily.   2. Motorcyclists—United States—Biography.
3. Motorcycles—Anecdotes.   4. Motorcycling.   I. Title.
GV1060.2.B757A3   2015   2014017320
796.75092—dc23
[B]

Printed in the United States of America
1   3   5   7   9   10   8   6   4   2

Book design by Meighan Cavanaugh

Names and identifying characteristics have been changed
to protect the privacy of the individuals involved.

Penguin is committed to publishing works of quality and integrity.
In that spirit, we are proud to offer this book to our readers;
however, the story, the experiences, and the words
are the author's alone.

For my parents

CONTENTS

MOTORCYCLES
I'VE LOVED

1.

Matter

I started learning about motorcycles when I was twenty-one. A friend was poring over a photo gallery of sleek, sexy sport bikes on his laptop, and I looked over his shoulder while he fantasized about buying one. Only passing time at first, I quickly found myself taking an interest in his research, egging him on to purchase something he couldn't possibly afford so that I could hop on the back and feel cool. I imagined myself doing this, but it was all guesswork—I hadn't been on a motorcycle since I was a little kid, when my dad used to prop me up on the gas tank of his dirt bike and take me up and down the driveway, my mother shouting after us to be careful as we sped away.

"That one," my friend said, as he settled on a black model with thick, silver exhaust pipes and a seat made for a jockey, slanted forward at an alarmingly steep angle. I was perplexed.

"But—where does the passenger sit?"

"They don't," he replied, and from that moment on I knew, without a doubt—I didn't want to be a passenger on someone else's motorcycle.

I wanted to be the one riding that motherfucker.

A FEW MONTHS BEFORE, I'd left a man I loved very much, one who had been my companion across four continents and throughout several years. In the process, I alienated almost everyone I knew in the Southern Hemisphere, lost my Australian residency visa, and abandoned one of my favorite people in the world. Making the choice to leave him was as devastating as it was necessary. I couldn't see myself anymore, could only make out our two-headed, two-hearted composite, a creature driven by compromise and safety. It was easy to live with Thom in Australia and feel as though I was being brave just by being fourteen time zones away from where I'd begun, but it took coming back to my beginning, to Vermont, to see that somewhere along the way I'd lost the intrepid thirst I'd started out with—and that I wanted it back.

A change in geography is a psychic jolt, like falling in love, or out of it, like doing drugs, or getting sober, like learning something new, or revisiting something forgotten. It's an electric pulse to the brain, but after the shock fades it's still the same brain, with the same thoughts and feelings and impulses. It's only a glimpse, a nudge toward what could be. An alarm going off, presenting the dreamer with a choice: between sleep and lucidity, stasis and change. I'd been hitting Snooze for so long, hopping from place to place, from person to person, hoping it would be enough, but it was only a series of false starts in exotic locales. Transformation takes sweat and tears; it can't be bought with a plane ticket or an admission of love.

At first the rubble in the wake of that one, abrupt decision to leave Thom overwhelmed me. The shock was dizzying, the wreckage seemingly insurmountable, but as I began picking up the pieces of a different life in New England, one I'd left behind at seventeen, I sensed possibility: more lives, yet to be lived. Work to do, room to grow. I'd put too much of my life force into someone else, had let the weight of my well-being rest on a single pillar in the center of my consciousness. When I let myself imagine what would happen if it all collapsed, I knew I had to do just that. Without the backdrop of Ireland or India or Australia, without Thom standing next to me, I could finally see myself, as if for the first time. I took stock. To find what was worth saving—and what wasn't.

It makes me think of the old barns and woodsheds along the Vermont country roads where I grew up, most of them in various degrees of disrepair, leaning at impossible angles for years, even decades. Ever so slowly disintegrating, season by season, defying all logic until finally the rotting, nail-bitten planks tilt too far in one direction and whatever beam had held it all together, whatever mystery had kept those walls from folding in, gives. A gust of wind, a heavy rain, and an empty meadow in the morning.

Time moves slowly in Vermont. Farmers leave it to the fields to take back the unused sugar shacks and empty wood-sheds—but I've never been so patient. I had to demolish in order to rebuild, and so I did it quickly, coldly. I couldn't wait for the ending to end, couldn't bear shrugging off the questions I didn't have answers to. A gutting drive to the bus station, Thom's backpack on his lap, fists resting on his thighs like grenades, a force field of confusion and tension buzzing between us. Only twenty minutes, yet an impossibly long trip, a strange, horrible good-bye muttered in the parking lot. We agreed that I would keep the car, he would keep the laptop, and we would close the joint bank account, then I set him loose—to make his own way back to Melbourne. There was a tang in the back of my throat as I drove away in the Corolla we'd bought together in California, the taste of battery acid and stale coffee and leftover love. And then, emptiness: an end and a beginning commingling in the dusty void.

WHEN I WAS SEVENTEEN I bought a backpack and a plane ticket, then wandered for three and a half years. I circled the globe: starting with Ireland, ending with Australia, joining hands in Vermont. During those years, I learned to pull a pint of stout, got robbed twice, made a fool of myself constantly, meandered through western Europe, fell in love, went to

India for a while, then gave Thailand a try; I kept moving, stopped moving, settled down in Melbourne, then started moving again. It was the sort of journey that forms a person, as surely all journeys during one's formative years do—it broke me apart, then built me back up again. I didn't recognize myself when I came home, didn't even know if *home* was the right word anymore, but at the very least, I knew I was made of something. Matter: I knew I was made of matter, which might not sound like much of a thing to know, but it's the only place to start.

If matter, that which has mass and occupies space, is the fabric of the universe, then energy is the thread that binds it together. In physics, it's relatively easy to understand ideas like this: to internalize the logic of matter and energy and the laws that follow, but the utter nonsense of being alive, of experiencing things and reacting to them, is murky, often distorted. The emotional landscape is archetypal and cryptic, and the cacophony of pink matter inside my skull seems to churn out nothing but noise. It can be hard to tell what's real—yet in physics I find clarity from time to time. I find scraps of order. Fleeting moments of comprehension.

Sometimes things come apart, irrevocably and inexplicably. When they do, it helps to go back to the beginning—the root of what is known. Assume nothing, test every plank, every nail. Return to the foundation, take it apart and look at the blocks. Turn them over in your hands, hold them. Then rebuild, slowly, carefully. Watch how they fit together. Matter.

Time. Speed. Distance. The less you think you know, the better off you are.

BACK IN NEW ENGLAND, I mourned my life in Australia and I began to build a new one, without having any idea of what I wanted it to look like. There were shadows of an earlier, younger self fluttering in the wings to contend with, and the jagged, raw edge where Thom and I had been connected, and the way nothing I knew about myself seemed to fit quite like it had before, my personality hanging on me like baggy jeans, a few sizes too big. I felt hollow, deflated, like there weren't enough organs in my chest, no blood in my veins. A vacuum the size of Australia, next to my beating heart. I had shrunk somehow, a withered soul living in an oversized vessel.

At some point I realized that empty space was what I'd needed all along. The chance to consider my own contents. To cull, reshape, and ultimately to innovate. To find stillness, and then, eventually, discover a new kind of motion.

2.

Acceleration

When I was a kid, my mother used to joke that she'd skin me alive if she ever caught me on the back of a motorcycle. Then, when I was seventeen, she told me she used to ride one. There was an Indian two-stroke, she said, with dusty black saddlebags and oily leather tassels that she rode from San Francisco to Missoula with a man she'd just met. They ran out of money in Washington and cleaned gas station bathrooms in exchange for the fuel to keep going. There was another bike she had, in Philadelphia, a Honda 305 that got stolen, boosted onto a truck in the middle of the night, and another in Vermont, an old Yamaha dirt bike she rode to her job as a public-school art teacher. She strapped a milk crate to the back and filled it with lesson plans and her lunch; it was 1981, and all the kids thought she was something else. I listened to my mother in awe as she counted off the motorcycles she'd owned and the motorcycles she'd ridden. She had me the same year she turned forty; I'd never known her young. She still taught art, but by then she was driving to school in a Toyota hatchback. There was a lot I didn't know.

I leaned forward and put my elbows on the countertop, and she told me how an old boyfriend taught her to ride his Triumph in an Illinois cornfield sometime during the mid-1960s, just before she dropped out of college. She'd ridden whiny little dirt bikes on the Jersey Shore as a teenager, but never a full-blooded motorcycle, and never with an engine like that—double-cylinder, four-stroke, *run home crying or ride straight to Las Vegas* polarity shimmering on the chrome finish.

I pictured it: pale green husks against indigo mountains that lay close to the earth, and the two of them, out there in a clearing by some ramshackle, whitewashed barn where the harvest was already cut and stacked. He taught her how to go, but before he could tell her how to stop she'd gone. The bike rumbled and she gunned it, showing off, thinking she had motorcycles down pat.

The front tire leapt into the air, the bike bucked her like a startled horse, and together they galloped forward: my mother, just barely hanging on to the throttle, inadvertently opening it up as far as it would go. She roared toward some hay bales, and when she couldn't swerve fast enough they caught her neatly, like rough pillows, plumped and piled high. I can see it: her boyfriend running to catch up to where she lay sprawled in the hay, overcome, laughing and sobbing and holding her arm like it had come apart at the elbow.

I love picturing my mother this way: with long dark hair and a leather jacket that's too big for her. I love thinking of her whipping down the highway, somewhere green and warm, a red handkerchief across her mouth to block the dust, and a big pair of mirrored aviators, pinned to her face by the wind. I wish she had been the one to show me how to ride, but there wasn't a chance in hell—I don't know how she taught me to drive a car without having a heart attack, but she's been telling me to slow down ever since.

THE MAN WHO did teach me to ride chewed the side of his oily thumb and looked me over: an overexcited twenty-one-year-old running my hands along the sleek lines of a cruiser, impatiently waiting for instructions. A clean V-neck T-shirt glowed white against the permanent grease smudges on his hands and the deep nut-brown of his arms, his black hair smoothed back into a ponytail. Back then he wasn't quite a friend yet—a friend of a friend—but he was a motorcycle man, and the only one I knew at the time. I had been running into him a lot lately, and pestering him about wanting to learn, until he'd finally succumbed and picked me up at the curb outside my house one afternoon. It was the first time I'd been on a motorcycle since I was a little kid clinging to the handlebars of my dad's dirt bike, but it felt familiar. We found a dirt road next to a sprawling farm in western Massachusetts to practice on.

The bike was borrowed, loaned by the motorcycle man's brother—a Yamaha Virago 750, I think. The engine was too much and the frame was too heavy for me at that point, but my feet could touch the ground and that was enough for me. I thought of my mother: sitting among the hay bales, four decades and a thousand miles away, but also somehow right next to me. On either side of the road, cornstalks were chopped low to the ground, and clouds were rolling in from across the river. A few drops of rain flecked my jacket. It was cold and getting late as I pressed the toes of my sneakers into the dirt, trying to master a machine that weighed four times as much as me. When it comes down to it, there are two ways to keep a motorcycle upright—by supporting its weight or by accelerating.

"Show me your gears," he said, and I dutifully kicked it into first, second, third, fourth, and fifth, then back to neutral.

"Show me your brakes," he said, and I squeezed the lever under my right hand.

"And your rear brakes?" I touched the pedal with my right foot.

"Good," he said. "Show me your throttle." I flicked my wrist and the engine came alive. "Now. Let's see what you got."

I felt the hum of 750cc's against the inside of my thigh and hot metal searing through the thick skin of my jeans—savage energy below me, literally combusting, over and over. Within the engine casing the pistons were firing away, like two empty syringes spurting exhaust instead of vaccine, compressing gas instead of liquid, workhorses shuttling back and forth, filling the chamber, compressing it, and exploding back in the other direction. From pistons to crankshaft to rear wheel, energy flowed until it became the motion in my tires and together we lunged forward.

The first moment of acceleration, when my feet lifted away from the road, buoyed up by the air itself, felt like leaving the ground completely. The weight of the bike dissipated into motion and it felt like ascension. As I straddled it in stillness, with my toes on the ground, it was deadweight, but when I let out the clutch and laid on the throttle, it lightened, became effortlessly balanced; it flew.

I pulled in the clutch, let go of the throttle, and knocked it up to second gear, then I accidentally jammed the throttle on so hard I slid back a few inches in my seat. Up to third, fourth, and the wind stung my neck, my knuckles. Ahead I could see deep, muddy ruts crisscrossing the road and no way around them. I hurried to rein in the engine, to bring it down gear by gear, but I hit the mud too soon and my back tire skidded onto its edge; my connection with the surface of the road slipped away. Instinctively, I tightened my fist on the brakes and the tires locked, the heaviness of stasis returned, and I lost momentum. Without it, I felt a few hundred pounds of churning metal begin to go down and to take me with it;

I stopped thinking about how to stay upright and started thinking about how to fall.

The engine died on impact, and even as I slithered out from underneath it I could feel the heat and the hum and the dull ache in my limbs that had begun to sharpen. I stood up and my ankle wobbled. My knee screamed, my palms were skinned raw, but I struggled to heave the bike back up. I took my helmet off and I tried again. The motorcycle man caught up to me, and together we pulled it up off the ground. He checked the bike over, decided it was okay; I checked myself over, couldn't decide.

THERE WAS ANOTHER STORY my mother told me, about another crash. This one was a little after she'd wiped out while she was learning in Illinois, in 1968 or so. She had just abandoned her sophomore year at Monmouth College and gone back to her parents' house in New Jersey while she figured out what to do next. In the meantime, she got an office job designing pamphlets at an insurance company and a blue Honda 305 cruiser to make life more interesting.

She had an old high school friend who had gotten into dirt bike racing, and one weekend the two of them and three other guys made the trip out to western Pennsylvania so that he could compete. The four guys rode in the van with the dirt bike, but my mother decided to ride her motorcycle. It was a beautiful day when they started out, a stubby little caravan of motocross misfits. The race itself was warm and sunny, but on the way home the weather turned. Rain began to bounce against her helmet and the sky darkened. She slowed down, tried to be careful, but she was tense, terrified of how easily she could lose control. There is a delicate ridge one must ride between fear and reason on a motorcycle—lean too far in either direction and there will be consequences.

They were on a winding road in the Pennsylvania mountains, twisting and turning their way down from the misty peak. The van followed her, and as she rounded a corner on a downward slope she braked and lost her traction on the wet asphalt. The wheels locked and slid out from under her. It was over in an instant. She laid the bike down, and together they slid to the shoulder of the road. The scrub grass caught her by the jacket, but the bike kept going. She lay there, a quivering, shaking mess, as the boys stopped the van and ran to her, shouting over the thrum of the rain against the road. Her left side ached from the impact, and she began to cry as they fussed over her, through gritted teeth, trying to will away each tear. They managed to fit her boxy little 305 into the van alongside the losing dirt bike, and they stowed her in the seat of honor, battered and aching from her battle with the road, then proceeded to give her the frame-by-frame replay of her crash the whole way back to New Jersey. She returned to her cubicle at the insurance company after the weekend, and her entire left side was a rainbow of bruises beneath her corporate-casual shell.

"LOOKIN' GOOD," the motorcycle man said after he saw I was just shaken up. I rubbed my knee and brushed mud from my pants. My hands were shaking and my heart was pumping like it might combust. He flicked the starter button and the engine turned over a few times before it caught. He revved it. "It's now or never," he said, and I knew what he meant. I hesitated, but I got on, and this time I found fifth gear out there among the shorn crops and the dry farm roads, the dust leaping up behind me like a banner.

DURING MY MOTORCYCLE safety course a month or so later, we practiced on a big square of asphalt in the middle of a field, way out by a tiny airport. There was a jumble of students: two teenage boys with crotch rockets who couldn't wait to get the hell out of there; two middle-aged women with long nails and dents on their ring fingers; an older, soft-voiced gentleman who used to ride as a young man and wanted to refresh his skills; and me. At twenty-one, I was done thinking about Australia, but I didn't know what to think about next. For months I had been in a state of shock, wondering what I had done, how I had managed to destroy everything that felt safe about my life with one well-aimed blow, and what I was supposed to do now. Thom was back in Melbourne, I'd found a place to live in Massachusetts, and time was creeping forward. I needed something to catch me up and catapult me out of the apathy that I was slowly settling into, but something more than an unfamiliar destination—I needed a new route, a different mode of travel. Returning to New England and leaving Thom had been intuitive. It gave me the foundation and the energy to expand as an individual, but the next part, doing that work and embracing that challenge, required effort and attention.

"Imagine there's a car in front of ya," our instructor, Joe, said. "And ya gotta stop real fast." He was a wiry little guy from the North Shore, with a sprout of black-and-gray hair and stubble that had been getting thicker all afternoon. I've never seen anyone more passionate about their job. He was crazy about motorcycles, and totally committed to the safety manual—those corny videos, even the pop quizzes at the end of every chapter. He wore an armored jacket and shiny, indestructible-looking pants, and he told us anyone who didn't wear a helmet was an asshole, no matter what state they lived in. He took a shine to me when I got a 100 on my written test, and when I started zipping around the practice tarmac on the little Kawasaki bike, he called me over, slapped me on the back, and laughed as he told me not to go too fast.

"Now the car in front of ya," Joe shouted, "is twenty yards away from ya—here." He scrubbed his toe against a white line painted on the asphalt. We were in a row, a ways off from him.

"And they've stopped real sudden. Now ya gotta get up to a good speed, then stop on the line." We nodded. We were ready. "Start your engines," he shouted. "Okay, Becky, c'mon down."

Becky's nails were hot pink and square tipped. She had on black leather knuckle gloves trimmed with tassels. She worked as a nurse, down at Hancock Regional, I think, and her ward was starting an all-women biker crew. She went, and it looked pretty good. Pretty simple. The teenagers went, too, and I admired their tire scorches. "Lily," Joe called to me, "all good to go." So I went.

In physics, the word *acceleration* means the rate of change in velocity—not necessarily an increase. A decrease in velocity is acceleration, too. The movement involved in stopping is the same kind of motion as getting up to speed. Consider an object moving in a straight line at a constant speed, then the same object at rest. The acceleration in both cases is zero, because it's the fluctuation of speed that is being measured, not the speed itself.

I jammed on my brakes. The sudden change jolted me forward and locked my back tire, but I kept the wheel straight and the front and rear brakes on evenly. I put my heels down, my front tire an inch or two shy of the line. On two wheels it's hard to remember to stomp down on the rear brake pedal and squeeze hard on the front with even, measured pressure, all the while committing to the change in velocity and, maybe more important, being ready to support the weight of the machine once it stops moving.

Joe strolled over and motioned for me to flip my visor up. "You know how fast you were goin'?" he asked, looking impressed. I shook my head, feeling pleased with myself, trying not to let it show. "Really freaking fast," he said. "But you stopped clean. You know why you ride just as good, prolly better than those boys over there?" he asked, and he jerked a thumb over at the hot-shit teenagers popping mini-wheelies near the shade tent.

"Why?" I asked.

"Because you got balls, kid."

"Huh," I said. "Thanks."

"That an' a fuckin' brain. One's no good without the other." He laughed and flipped my visor back down, then gave me a resounding smack on the top of my helmet.

Riding that ridge between reason and recklessness, stillness and speed, is the first, maybe the most important, thing I learned about motorcycles. It's a balance I'd never fully understood in any setting. I experimented with both extremes, in Ireland, hitchhiking on rural roads, taking rides from just about anyone; or in India, refusing to walk to the bazaar alone, making Thom go instead. As a woman traveling by herself I'd confused bravery with stupidity, and as a woman in a partnership I'd confused caution with cowardice. It's an equilibrium that takes practice, but on a motorcycle there's not much room for interpretation—some things are just easier to learn when the pavement is keeping score.

"Now," Joe said, "go do it again."

3.

Force

I had been casually scanning the local motorcycle classifieds for weeks, but when I finished the safety course and
passed the riding test I began to search in earnest, shutting
myself in my room for hours at a time to sift through motorcycle listings. I had lived in western Massachusetts for almost
a year by then, in a town called Northampton, waiting tables
in a French restaurant and partying hard, with a constant rotation of five to six other housemates.

My life in Australia was still vivid, but the details of my old
routine had begun to feel distant: riding the train to the city
center each morning, walking through Carlton Gardens in
flip-flops, high heels stowed in my shoulder bag. Eight-hour
days spent at a boutique market-research firm, answering the
phone, helping the researchers with their reports, leading focus
groups into comfortable rooms where their reactions could be

watched and recorded from behind a one-way mirror. Then arriving home a little past six, making dinner, feeding the cat, and later watching television while Thom did the dishes.

Thom and I stayed in touch after we broke up and he returned to Australia. He would send me packages with some of my belongings now and then, a box of clothes, some old letters, a stack of photos. Every time something arrived with an Australian postmark I would sit on my bed and cry. We talked on the phone a few times, e-mailed occasionally. We discussed the possibility of getting back together someday, and while it was earnest at the time, I see now that it was always an empty plan, grasping at straws to damp down the distress of being so far apart and the very real prospect that we would never see each other again.

Although memories of Australia were slowly receding, my current life had yet to sharpen. The ground I stood on felt shaky. I was still expanding, accumulating matter, waiting for my ambitions to materialize and then solidify. The plan with Thom had included a permanent-residency visa and going back to school in Melbourne, but without Thom and without Australia, there was no plan. I still wanted to finish my bachelor's degree but didn't know what to study or where to apply—all I knew was I didn't want to feel lost anymore. I wanted a direction, but I didn't want to keep drifting to find it. The physical motion of my travels began to seem more evasive than transformative. I knew there had to be a way to move forward without buying a plane ticket.

It didn't help that almost as soon as I had decided to stay in New England, my parents decided to leave. They sold the house in Vermont where I grew up and moved to Florida, where my father could work outdoors all year round and my mother could continue teaching online college classes but retire from public school, exploring a whole new gardening climate in her free time. After thirty years of hard Vermont winters, they were ready for a change. I understood their reasons for going but was dismayed to lose my childhood home. It seemed like I'd just returned, and already I was packing up my old room, inheriting the furniture and carpets and appliances they didn't want to transport south.

I grew up in a beautiful, unusual house with tall, expansive windows, my father's woodshop on the first floor, our home on the second, set on a hill in the middle of a spacious meadow, acres of forest all around. My parents designed and built it together, the art teacher and the carpenter each playing to their strengths. The view of it from the bottom of our driveway, my mother's gardens sprawled on every side, was rustic and elaborate all at once: a grand gray-blue barn with a silo, a weather-vane shaped like a rooster spinning on the peak of its roof. I had never planned on living there again, but when they sold it and went south I felt more adrift than ever. I ached for an anchor, a place to call home.

For a time, the house in Northampton was that anchor, and although it never quite felt like home, it kept me occupied. Something was always happening at the house on North

Street: a stew being cooked; a show being played; a dinner being eaten; a dog visiting, or a small child, or an old friend; a noise band sleeping on the floor; a yard sale out front: a traffic jam in the driveway. We never locked the doors, because there was always someone home, and we never bought bread, because there was always someone living there who worked at the Hungry Ghost bakery and brought home the day-old loaves. It was a transient way to live—the house was for sale the entire time I was there—but that felt okay. After bouncing around the globe, I no longer felt the need to constantly be on the move, but as much as I craved a home, I wasn't ready to stop completely, to let the dust settle and commit, so it was a good compromise. I was on the verge of something, a new adventure, a stretch of fresh terrain, but I had yet to find the right vehicle to take me over the brink.

I had only two specifications within my modest price range: at five-foot-three, I wanted a motorcycle with a frame low enough for my feet to comfortably touch the ground, and with enough force in the belly of its engine to be taken seriously.

Since I have always looked both younger and smaller than I feel, being taken seriously has often felt like an uphill battle, with my anatomy fighting for the other side. For years the word *cute* has been robbing me of my dignity; even my anger seems to inspire the same reaction toddlers receive. When I raise my voice it goes up an octave, and when I want to get the salad bowl down from the cupboard I need a chair to reach it.

At fifteen I got a job as a waitress, then promptly lost it when they realized I was too young to serve alcohol, and when I started traveling at seventeen I was constantly scolded, told over and over again that the world was just not safe for a girl like me to be all on her own, as if I wasn't strong enough or smart enough or bold enough to take care of myself. To this day, people I don't even know sometimes insist I don't look a day over sixteen—as if this is what women in their twenties want to hear.

People implied or just flat out told me I was too young, too fragile, or too small so often I bought it. As an adolescent I could never quite reconcile this discrepancy between who I wanted to be and who I appeared to be. I began to think being cute was the only way I could have any power at all, and although I've never liked that aspect of myself—that part of me that is willing to cash in on the doe eyes and the blood that flushes my cheeks red-hot at the slightest provocation—I went with it. It felt like my only weapon.

Learning to travel, to make my way in the world, shifted this perception, and then learning to ride motorcycles shattered it completely. People looked at me a little differently when I arrived in leather, on two wheels, and it made me begin to look at myself differently, too. I remembered that I'm not this undersized shell, or at least I don't have to be—I have a choice. When I see myself now, my shoulders are broad enough to fill an elevator, my hands are big like dinner plates, and I can reach anything I damn please. My voice is low and gravelly, my skin rough and grooved by the elements, tough as alligator meat. I am ancient—old and wise and stoic, like a giant sea turtle that swings herself up out of the sea every now and then to see the young, pink sunbathers, then sinks back down below to sleep in the sand. But it doesn't change the fact that in the mirror I'm just this little piece of pale, blue-eyed fluff who looks as though she might blow away in heavy winds. At first I struggled to reconcile the reality of my mind's eye with my reflection. I wanted the force I felt welling up inside me to be apparent to everyone. I wanted it to show on my face.

In physics, force is an influence that causes a free body to undergo a change in velocity or a change in shape. It's a fundamental concept in Newtonian mechanics—the foundation for everything that comes after. In conversation, force is synonymous with strength or power. Both the physical and the metaphysical facets of force inhabit the world of motorcycles: the force provided by the engine, and the force provided by the rider. For decades motorcycles have been symbols of power, transforming anyone at the handlebars into a demigod of the road through sheer imposition: the rumbling exhaust, the thumping engine, the glittering chrome, the studs and the leather. The motorcycle itself is the avenue for literal, mechanical force, but its rider is the apex of its strength, the crest of its power. I think of oiled black hide, hidden faces, heavy boots; I think of long, empty roads and dark, close streets and saddlebags packed for anything that might lie in between. I think of the motorcyclist as an archetype: the lone rider, or the restless soul, rolling through seedy towns like a tumbleweed until the wind catches her up and carries her back out to the desert to spin in the dunes.

ONCE I GOT my new license in the mail, marked with an *M* for *motorcycle*, I doubled the time I spent haunting the motorcycle classifieds, Googling models and makes until they ran together in one long, metallic streak. I retreated to my bedroom and shut the door more and more often, growing tired of all the hanging out that transpired on the other side of the wall, beginning to feel a rift widening, my bedroom breaking away from the house like an ice floe and drifting downriver. The years I had spent traveling were all blank pages to my friends—I had simply disappeared for a time, and then one day returned. At first, as I tried to numb the grief and the guilt I felt over leaving Thom, this suited me, but as the months wore on I began to realize I was regressing rather than advancing. I was acting like my seventeen-year-old self, pretending those years hadn't happened. I was perpetually drunk or stoned, but ideally both, smoking a pack of cigarettes a day although I'd quit around the same time I'd met Thom, stumbling through a series of events and calling it fun.

When I discovered motorcycles, roughly a year after I'd returned to the United States, it was the first time since I'd made the decision to leave Thom that my sense of adventure was stirred, my curiosity aroused. It was the feeling I had been looking for all along. It reminded me of the power I'd felt when I bought my plane ticket to Ireland four years before, the tremors that had set the tectonics of my consciousness in motion, and when I felt those tremors again I knew I was finally doing something right.

I went to look at one motorcycle, a dud, then arranged to see another. On the way, I picked up my friend Rigdhen, the man who had taught me to ride out in the meadows, and threw a pack of American Spirits into his lap in exchange for his expertise. He lit one for me and one for himself, and together we found the address on some tiny dead-end drive on the Northampton/Easthampton border. Rigdhen fiddled with the motorcycle in question and talked shop with the guy selling it as I looked on, trying to seem seasoned or knowledgeable, and failing miserably. The bike began to smoke a little when we started it and sounded like a dying animal. Rigdhen gave me this look, like, *Nice going,* and I shrugged at him, as in, *What the fuck do I know.* We left shortly thereafter. I brought Rigdhen back to the garage where he worked and we sat on the hood of my car for a minute before he went in. He assured me there would be other motorcycles.

"There's a Rebel 250 in Waltham," I said, summoning hope and remembering the ad I had been looking at earlier. I was still hung up on wanting something a little bigger—400 or 500cc's, maybe, but by then impatience had won out. I had gotten my license and saved the money. I wasn't interested in shopping wisely, or in waiting for a certain look, a great bargain, or even a smart investment. I wanted to be on two wheels by Friday. Rigdhen raised an eyebrow and shook his head slightly.

"I don't think I know where Waltham is."

"Me neither," I said. He considered for a moment, and smoked the rest of his cigarette in one long drag before flicking it into the bushes and hopping off the hood. The metal made a loud pop as it shifted back into its usual shape.

"I guess I'll bring the van, then," he said, and loped inside with a backward wave.

A few days later we cruised down the Mass Pike, *Car Talk* on the radio, a bag of salt-and-vinegar potato chips between us. We were on the hunt for Waltham, ready to haul the bike back with us in the big, white painter's van if the sale went through. Rigdhen tried to temper my excitement for the purchase, but without success; I was already determined that, barring catastrophe, the van would not be empty on the ride home.

I looked out the window while Rigdhen told me about the new yoga teacher he was dating, and then we talked about the other yoga teacher, whom he was no longer dating. We talked about India, where Rigdhen grew up, and Tibet, where his parents are from. He told me he liked to paint—murals, mostly. The conversation drifted; we turned up the radio when "Born to Be Wild" came on and decided it was a good omen. Touching the swell of cash in my pocket, I checked the directions again, not wanting to miss the exit. We did, of course, but after a few wrong turns and some backtracking we managed to arrive at the address only a few minutes late. The man selling the Rebel was waiting for us when we pulled up, and as we got out and shook hands he didn't say much, just twitched his gray mustache in my direction and pointed at the electric-blue motorcycle parked in the driveway. He was a little guy, with his plaid shirt tucked into his jeans and his belt done up real tight. His wife floated in and out of the garage without ever speaking to us directly, and a grown son leaned up against the wall, looking sullen. It was the wife's bike, we learned, and she was trading up for a Nighthawk 450, already bought and parked just inside. I couldn't help but fawn over the Nighthawk a little; it was, after all, the exact thing I had been looking for, but her smaller Rebel sister was the reason we had driven all this way.

Rigdhen confirmed that all was reasonably well with the Rebel after some tinkering. We tried knocking the price down, but the seller was firm. "She's worth it," he said, and the simplicity of his conviction was enough to end the haggling. I was hesitant because of how small the Rebel seemed, but then I realized that this instinctual connection between size and force was exactly what I was trying to disprove. I wanted a bigger bike so that I would, by association, be more forceful, but then I realized we matched, she and I, our strength hidden away beneath an unlikely exterior, and so I gave him the money and he gave me the title. Rigdhen rode it up a metal ramp and into the back of the van, where we strapped it down, and then we all shook hands again. In the sideview mirror I saw the man give us a loose salute as we took off, and then he went back inside. Rigdhen drove; I folded the title twice and put it in my pocket. The dashboard glowed orange in the glare of a quickly sinking sun, and as we swung out onto the highway I couldn't help but look over my shoulder at the Rebel every now and again, peeking out of the darkness, her big, luminous headlight staring back at me, and the sunset reflected in her gaze, warm and golden.

I could barely sit still the whole way back to Northampton. When we finally arrived and unloaded the Rebel from the van, it was dark. We parked it in the driveway and shared a can of beer as we admired the glow of chrome from the porch steps. Rigdhen went home after the beer was gone, but I stayed outside, turning the Rebel on now and then to hear the roar, then reluctantly turning it off again, counting the hours until the Registry of Motor Vehicles office would open and I could get it on the road.

MOTORCYCLES ARE usually referred to by the size of their engines, and the unit of measurement is most often the cc, or cubic centimeter, although on American motorcycles you'll see this number expressed in cubic inches. The measurement refers to the capacity of the engine, or, in mechanical terms, the engine's displacement: the amount of air and fuel that is swept into an engine during one complete cycle. Once the chamber is full and the piston has been pushed from the top down to the bottom by the intake, the piston compresses the mixture until it is ignited, the explosion of which forces the piston back to its original place as the chamber fills once again and the process is repeated. The size of the chamber correlates with the size of the combustion, which is at the root of an engine's force output.

Whether there is one cylinder or six, an internal combustion engine will work in essentially the same way, but the more cylinders you have, the more volume your engine can handle, and therefore the more force it can generate. Between a 125cc dirt bike with a single cylinder and a 6,000cc Boss Hoss cruiser packing eight, there's quite a scope of power to consider. The size of an engine is, of course, relative to how much force it outputs, but that's not the whole story. An engine needs to be tuned in order to produce maximum power. The idle speed, fuel/air mixture, carburetor balance, and ignition timing each play a part in how the engine performs, and while knowing an engine's displacement might give an idea as to what kind of power is available, in the end cc's are a measurement of volume—not force.

With regard to vehicles, horsepower is the unit of measurement used most often to describe an engine's force output, but the relationship between horsepower and cc's is indefinite. A 125cc engine tuned for maximum power can generate as much as 50 horsepower, whereas the same engine, tuned differently, might get only 20 hp. Racing vehicles are where the strongest ratio between engine displacement and horsepower can be found, because speed is the one and only goal, but some of the weakest ratios can be found in the largest engines, where endurance and stability are most desired. A ship's engine with fourteen cylinders, weighing roughly 2,300 tons, has a displacement of 25,498,000 cubic centimeters but generates only 108,920 horsepower. It seems like a big number, but proportional to its displacement, it's not all that impressive. Then consider a tiny 3.5cc model car engine, and get this: it can generate up to 3.45 hp. Now, that *is* impressive, whether the kid holding the remote control knows it or not. Size and force are relative, but there is so much more to it.

ON MONDAY I DISCOVERED, after waiting on a bench at the RMV for an hour and a half, that the registration fees for the Rebel would be more than a hundred bucks and only personal checks or cash were acceptable forms of payment. I squeezed seventy-six dollars out of my wallet and a little pile of change from my pockets before I admitted defeat and left the teller's window in dejection. I made my way out to the parking lot and circled the block, fuming with frustration, looking for an ATM so that I could withdraw the very last of the money I had managed to save from waiting tables all year and had set aside for acquiring a motorcycle.

When I got back to the RMV, cashed up and calmed

down, I slipped past the waiting masses to the woman I had been speaking to earlier, ignoring the dirty looks shot my way. She took my money and my forms, then handed me a full-sized set of license plates in a wax-paper bag and waved me off, shooing me away like a fly. I laughed nervously, and she gave me a look. We stared at each other for a second.

"Um," I said, and then paused, trying to be diplomatic, not wanting to point out her mistake. She waited, obviously irritated. "These are for a motorcycle?"

She checked the forms and a flood of apologies emerged; she became almost sweet.

"I'm so sorry," she said, "I wasn't even paying attention. These wouldn't fit, huh?"

"Ha. No, I guess they wouldn't."

"Let me get you the right kind." She disappeared for a moment and returned with a single plate, about the size of my hand. "Does this look a little better?"

"It does." I nodded.

She smiled, but there was something sad about it. "I used to ride on the back of my husband's Harley," she told me, as if the husband and the bike were both distant memories. "I loved it." She had beautiful cheekbones magnified by enormous glasses frames. I imagined her in leathers, a decade or two younger, her arms wrapped around the waist of the faceless husband, roaring through some quiet rural town. She looked past me, and I wondered if we were imagining the same thing. I thanked her, and before I walked away I leaned across the counter for a second, palms flat on the cool plastic surface.

"You should get your own," I said, "sans husband."

She laughed and shooed me away. "You're cute," she said and sighed. "If I was a young thing like you, maybe I would." Before I could respond, the number over her station clicked forward and a mother carrying her toddler under one arm squeezed past me. I wanted to tell her what I had only begun to learn for myself: That she had a choice. That there's no such thing as too old or too young, no such thing as too small, or too weak. We tell children that they can be whoever they want to be when they grow up, but then forget we can make that choice as adults, too. A motorcycle is a vehicle of change, after all. It puts the wheels beneath a midlife crisis, or a coming-of-age saga, or even just the discovery of something new, something you didn't realize was there. It provides the means to cross over, to transition, or to revitalize; motorcycles are self-discovery's favorite vehicle.

When I got home I attached the license plate to the Rebel's fender with a few zip ties and took her out for our first ride together. I went around the block a few times to smooth out my shifting, and then we leapt out onto Route 9, amid the humming traffic. I weaved around potholes and frost heaves, and when I rolled up to a stoplight I revved the engine joyfully while waiting for it to turn green. I could almost see that archetypal motorcyclist up ahead, hair lashing out behind her like a banner, her spurs sharpened to razor points and her hand heavy on the throttle. She took her turns low to the ground and flew between passing cars, tires eating up the dotted line, a speeding smudge of silver and black.

About an hour later, I pulled into my garage and cut the engine. I got off and stepped back to admire the fiery blue glow of my gas tank in the dim light. A friend of a friend glided up the driveway on his bicycle and stopped to admire the Rebel with me for a moment. "It's so cute," he said, and I frowned, dissatisfied for a moment, in his reaction and in my purchase, but then I stopped myself short. After years of letting that word diminish me, I reminded myself that it was only a word: a house-trained, second-rate adjective that had about as much potency behind it as *fine* or *cool*. Maybe it was true, and so what if it was? It wasn't his reaction that mattered, it was mine.

"Yeah," I agreed. "She is." Suddenly, I didn't care if the force I felt showed on my face; I knew it was there. It would have to be enough.

4.

Velocity

Velocity is a word that's often used interchangeably with speed, but it's more specific than that. It's not only the rate of speed but also the direction that it travels in. It's a vector property, which is to say that its definition includes both a magnitude and a direction. On the other hand, speed is a scalar because it defines only a quantity. Sixty miles per hour is a speed. Sixty miles per hour, heading south, is a velocity.

My older brother, Phineas, used to play this computer game called *Escape Velocity*, and as I was hardly a worthy gaming adversary, I would often just sit and watch him play. This was in the mid-nineties, so the graphics weren't complex; you, the little spaceship in the middle of the screen, were traveling through outer space very, very fast. There was debris in your way, and sometimes other spaceships shot sluggish laser beams at you. You could land on planets and develop trade relationships with their governments, and you could flip on your hyperdrive to travel instantaneously between stars. I remember rolling the name around in my mouth, *Escape Velocity*, thinking maybe it had something to do with going faster than the speed of light, never really being sure.

Later I learned that *escape velocity* is a scientific term—but it's a misnomer, as it quantifies a speed independent of direction. It should probably be called *escape speed*, but that just doesn't have the same ring to it. Escape velocity refers to the minimum speed required to break free, or to escape, from gravity, and it can be in any direction. I guess that's where the name of the computer game comes from: jumping from planet to planet, breaking free from gravity over and over again. It's an inspiring idea: you, that little spaceship, overcoming powers as great as a planet's gravitational pull, mission after mission, defying the sway of the universe and sallying forth into empty, unexplored space; blasting through the barrier. When I think of it that way, I understand my brother a little better—he was always searching for a way to escape gravity, never mind the direction of the trajectory.

When he was twenty-three he found it. All it took was a broken heart and a solo cross-country drive. I didn't see him for more than seven years. He went to Utah first, and found God, then to Washington, and found conspiracies. He signed over his bank account, his soul, and his station wagon to fundamental Christians and then either alienated or ignored everyone he had ever known.

Phin left right around my fourteenth birthday, and after a few months of silence, I began to receive letters from him at boarding school. They were hard to follow, full of half-finished thoughts and scribbles crammed onto both sides of tattered sheets of college-ruled paper. He called me a sinner and an ignorant fool and told me I was going to end up in hell. He told me my parents were criminals, that we were sleep-walkers, and that my only hope of salvation was to throw myself upon the mercy of God. Confused and devastated, I read and reread each one, looking for some glimmer of logic, of familiarity. I didn't find any. His slingshot away from the early years sent him off on a trajectory so drastic he seemed like another person. He still does, but the shock and the nostalgia has worn away to the meager thread of our shared childhood. These days, I try to rein our interactions in to the mundane and keep the connection alive, but the neutral ground left to us is scant. Another way to think of velocity is as the rate of displacement—how quickly and in what way an object moves away from its original place.

WE GREW UP IN RURAL VERMONT, and we both went to the local school, which educated kindergarten through eighth grade. There were about sixty or seventy students who went there. The older kids went to the high school in the next town over, and there was just one year that Phineas and I rode the bus to school together. Me, a tiny kindergartner clinging desperately to his huge eighth-grader hand. I remember him zipping up my coat for me during the winter and making me wear my hat even when I didn't want to, shepherding me into my classroom in the mornings. The year after, he was on a different bus, at a different school, but I remember waiting at the bottom of the hill together in the mornings, hands in our pockets as we leaned out into the road, trying to spot a bus coming around the bend. Sometimes we would leave a nickel on the guardrail post and check to see if it was still there when we got home.

There is a photo of us around this age that I've carried during all my travels and pinned to the wall in each of my homes. He's fourteen or so. I am five or six. He leans his head back against an Adirondack chair painted pale blue and looks at the camera. His Adam's apple is exposed, just beginning to swell with adolescence, and his childish black bowl cut is tousled. He smiles, mischievously. I am a golden blur on his right, the profile of my delighted features visible beside a curtain of moving hair. I am whispering a secret in his ear and he is surreptitiously tickling me just as the shutter clicks, making me shriek with laughter.

About the same time this was taken, my dad bought a hunter-green 125cc dirt bike for eighty dollars and taught my brother how to ride it. They would go to an abandoned gravel pit up the road to practice—popping wheelies among the sand dunes, taking jumps off the diminished gravel piles. I was so young—I can't tell which memories are real and which are built from secondhand stories, but I can remember impatiently waiting my turn to take a ride on my father's lap, zipping up and down the dirt road we lived on. He had this dark brown leather bomber jacket with a faux fur collar that he wore all throughout the nineties, and big horn-rimmed glasses that, in league with his beard, took over his entire face. I remember holding on to the handlebars with my tiny fists, the fur collar on his jacket tickling the back of my neck, sitting on his lap with my short little legs humming against the gas tank and watching the road flow by beneath us—or at least I think I do.

The bike didn't last long. Maybe a year or two, then my brother crashed it in the meadow behind our house. Phin would have been thirteen or fourteen, and totally incapable of following anything resembling direction. The grass was tall and slippery, and there was a rock he just couldn't see. It must have been a big one, because when he hit it he was launched high into the air. I think of him hovering for a moment before crashing down, long limbs flopping, back arched against the sky, and for a split second gravity couldn't touch him. He'd been told over and over not to ride on the grass—even I knew he wasn't supposed to—but he didn't care.

My father was furious. The membrane that seems to shield most people's emotions from their impulses is extraordinarily thin in my dad. He has always been an all-or-nothing kind of man—usually brimming with love, occasionally overflowing with rage. The incident with the motorcycle was only one of many conflicts between him and my brother. He hauled the bike into the shed and sold it the first chance he got. Game over. Phin ended up with some bruises and a burn on his calf from the muffler when he crashed. I remember admiring it: the flaking skin, the shiny mottled pucker around the edges. It was a beauty. I revered his recklessness, his loosely focused tenacity, but most of all his battle scar. I wanted one just like it.

I HAD A SENSE of never quite being able to catch up to my brother. I was forever stuck in this body that was too small for my aspirations—I wanted to be a sidekick, or a cohort, anything but his dumb kid sister. When Phin was in high school, the pedestal I set him on was so high I could barely see him up there. I thought everything he did was fantastic, even when it wasn't, and although he'd been my protector when I was very young, as a teenager he lost interest in me, then became my tormentor instead. I was annoying, and precocious, and an exact opposite of him in a hundred ways, a fact that seemed to grate on him the older we got, but that served only to fascinate me more and more. He was lanky and brooding, getting taller by the second, with black hair and a troubled soul, struggling through school, clashing with my father constantly. I was tiny and golden, always smiling, always hovering too closely at his elbow, breezing through my elementary years in a way that I see now must have been infuriating, charming my parents into taking my side whenever there was a gray area. I sensed a certain bitterness coming from him, as if I had no right to learn so easily or to smile so brightly, but this only made me more indebted to him, more resolved to earn his love, his respect.

In earlier years, my brother was my ally whenever our parents fought. He would stay with me in my room, the covers tented over our heads, while they shouted on the other side of the wall. He would tell silly jokes and make faces until the shouting died down and the apologies had been made. Then, as a teenager, he became the adept instigator of these explosions. His "bad attitude" was the constant culprit, and I would seek refuge alone, from all three of them. He got a car when he was sixteen, and from then on he was rarely home. His absences were easier in a lot of ways, but I never stopped missing him.

I don't mean to be stingy, I have beautiful memories, too: my brother and my father playing catch with a Frisbee, and me running between them, hopelessly trying to intercept it, utterly thrilled to be a part of their game. The pair of rabbits we bought at a farmer's market one year, that we thought were both boys but turned out to be one of each, and the dozens of accidental bunnies that followed, too many for the hutch we kept them in. And the cats, of course, a constant rotation that were always disappearing into the woods and reappearing weeks later. The cats would stalk the birds, I would stalk the cats, and my brother would stalk me. No one could make me laugh quite so hard, or scream quite so loud, as Phineas could. I remember once he startled me so badly I burst into tears, and he spent an entire afternoon trying to make it up to me.

As family lore tells it, I was an easy baby. In contrast, Phin's reign of terror is legendary. There is one story in particular that always comes to mind, in which he and my mother are in a grocery store—Phin is four, maybe five—and he reaches for a sugary cereal. She says no. In protest, he lies down on the dirty tile floor, screaming his heart out, until my mother is forced to throw him over her shoulder like a sack of potatoes, gather up her purse, and abandon the cart amid stares and raised eyebrows, carrying him out to the parking lot.

Phineas was undoubtedly difficult, but I loved that about him. His complexity, his epic disdain for stupidity and pop culture and redneck politics, the pendulum effect of his moods—all of this seemed unbelievably exciting. More than that, though, was his ability to react without thinking. I was a child consumed with hesitation, but he was all action. No analysis, no false starts, just the plunge: headfirst. I couldn't understand how he did it, but I knew I wanted to learn how. There were so many bold adventures in his repertoire—riding dirt bikes, going spelunking in West Virginian caves with my father, being fantastic in productions like *The Odd Couple* and *The Real Inspector Hound* and *Guys and Dolls*. In one play, he was cast as an old, wild-eyed, fire-and-brimstone-style preacher. I remember finding that particular transformation—the white paint in his hair, the fury of his declarations, the zeal on his face—remarkable.

I couldn't wait to arrive at that age of privilege and independence, to stop being the spectator and start learning the game, but when I eventually got there, Phineas might as well have been on a different planet. He went to college in northern Vermont for a year, then dropped out and moved to Boston—I would have been ten or eleven. Suddenly, he was no longer in my orbit. I went to visit him in Boston a few glorious times, but it was like visiting the moon. I knew I didn't get to stay.

When I was nine, before he moved, I remember driving around in his car, a two-door piece of junk he called the Rusty Justy, listening to mix tapes. It was a rare moment in those years that he was paying attention to me, and I was alert to everything about it: the fast-food wrappers at my feet, the smell of his cigarette and the overflowing ashtray, the grumble of the engine, the grayness of the light coming through the windshield. An early White Stripes song came on, consisting of two lines and some *whoa-oh-oh-ohs* thrown in:

> *When I hear my name, I want to disappear . . .*
> *When I see my face, I want to disappear*

Phineas let the song finish and then he turned off the tape. "Do you ever feel that way?" he asked me.
"What way?" I said.

"Like you wanna disappear."

"Oh." I thought for a minute, immediately wondering what he wanted to hear, even before I'd fully digested the question. "Yeah. I do," I said, then began worrying I'd given him the wrong answer. "Do you?"

"Yeah," he said and nodded. "All the time." Then he turned on the tape again and we didn't talk anymore. We didn't need to. I felt slightly less alone, and I like to think he did, too.

WHEN HE ACTUALLY did disappear, I felt more alone than ever. He left to go on his cross-country road trip a few weeks before the beginning of my freshman year, and after several months of silence I began to receive his letters. Phin's displacement became an obsession I had no room for, but which I clung to anyway. He had been my idol for so long, I couldn't give him up. It was like a nightmare in which I was holding something inanimate and cuddly, a doll or a stuffed animal, and suddenly it became a snapping, shrieking monster with sharp teeth and huge jaws. For a few years I couldn't manage to reconcile myself to this new reality. I kept trying to say something, anything, that would make him snap out of it and become himself again. I started thinking of myself as an only child because I didn't know how else to understand where my co-conspirator had gone, never mind how to articulate it. I just knew I had to let him go, that while I was wait-ing for the monster in my hands to change back into a teddy bear, it was ripping me apart.

I grew up and went on my own journey, disappeared in my own way. Eventually, I let go of the boy I remembered so vividly. The fixation of my teenage years gave way to a fero-cious grudge I sustained for more than half a decade. Long after Phineas had extended the olive branch, I stayed silent. I finally went to visit him out west and met the man he had become when I was twenty-one and he was thirty, seven years after I'd watched him drive away. His face was a little fuller, his beard and his waistline a little thicker. My mother always used to refer to him as a string bean when he was a teenager, but he had lost his gangly scrawniness and become a sol-id-looking man, handsome, with broad shoulders and wire-rimmed glasses. He told me he was a line cook and worked the graveyard shift in a fast-food kitchen, which he liked be-cause he had the whole line to himself, and that he studied the Bible in his free time. He said he didn't have many friends; that he didn't want many. We talked about our parents. There were so many memories of my childhood that I had never fully understood, and here was my chance. "I'll tell you when you're older" was the line I had been used to hearing, and here I was, finally: older. It was the first time we had spoken as adults, and there was so much I wanted to know.

We went for a walk, using fallen branches to switch away

the mosquitoes from our bare legs, taking pictures here and there because my mother had demanded it with an intensity I don't often see in her. It was the first time in seven years that her two children had been in the same state, and she wouldn't let it go undocumented.

He pointed out the chemtrails in the sky, wispy puffs of chemicals sprayed by clandestine government airplanes. I nodded, but my heart was sinking as he became animated, explaining about the Them that seemed to dominate his entire life; I didn't press for details. Thom and I stayed for a few more days, in a motel not far from Phin's house, where he rented a room and slept on the floor in a sleeping bag. Phin and I did our best to tiptoe around the land mines, each of us thinking the other was crazy, silently agreeing not to mention it. "Let me know when you're ready to wake up from your illusions," he whispered to me sometime before I left, and although I knew he meant it kindly, I was furious. Furious at him for being recognizable but indelibly different, for not understanding what he had done to me, and to our family, to my parents; furious at him for his staunch conviction that I was the one who needed waking up.

I drove away that day not knowing when I would see him again but needing to feel the wind lashing around the open windows of the car, the highway slipping away beneath my feet, never mind the destination. I needed to move. Phineas and I travel at different velocities, but I understand his impulse for motion, because I feel it, too.

. . .

I FELT THAT SAME IMPULSE about a year later, when a man I was interested in started sleeping with someone else. I had ridden up to the northwestern border of Massachusetts to work at a youth camp, just weeks after buying the Rebel, and I learned about the affair from some gossipy campers, who re-counted their after-hours discovery with delight, not knowing I would care—but I did care. The stress of working with teen-agers twenty-four hours a day, of living in a mildewed tent, of feeling that unexpected stab of rejection, suddenly over-whelmed me.

It seems trivial now, but in that moment the elusive prom-ise of perspective in a week, a day, even an hour, was utterly useless. I felt exhausted, angry, spurned, and something came loose inside of me—what was that, I wondered, logic? Calm? But it was too late, I was moving, and I didn't care what had come loose, would have shaken my entire fucking head like a piggy bank if I could have, until it all fell out, every last thought, every last emotion. The pressure that built inside my chest propelled me toward my helmet in the staff room, then down to the parking lot, slamming doors, stomping my feet, kicking rocks the whole way. I felt hurt, and with that came a slow simmer of unhinged, senseless rage in the pit of my stomach. Some sliver of my consciousness panicked, grasped for logic, for perspective, but there was none.

Rage is an emotion that I rarely display in the company of

others, and that has always frightened me in other people; I've seen it redden the faces of the men in my family far too often, contorting their familiar features into warped versions of themselves, suddenly and inexplicably transforming a father or a brother into a monster. I remember the terror a raised voice would instill in me, how I would cover my head with my arms as if the volume would physically hurt me. My memories of their wrath rarely make sense to me, even now: my father losing his shit because I didn't line up my shoes, my brother shaking me so hard my teeth rattled because I borrowed one of his comic books. My own rage is buried deep—as a child, I would go to my room, shut the door, and throw pillows when I felt angry, never able to lose myself enough to forget the consequences of destruction. Phineas, on the other hand, never even seemed aware of the consequences. I inflicted the rage I felt on myself, quietly and brutally, but Phin projected his onto the whole world, without provocation or mercy.

I GOT TO THE PARKING LOT, just beyond the boundaries of the camp, where I was keeping my motorcycle underneath a tarp, the corners tucked through the spokes of the tires to hold it down, a big rock pinning it to the seat. I ripped the tarp off and flung it into the scrubby grass, and the rock rolled underneath a car. I took the tiny key from my pocket, opened the choke, and pressed the starter button.

As soon as the engine coughed to life, the tightly coiled

tendons in my neck loosened a little; my shoulders began to sink. Just hearing the thump of the combustion, the wheeze of the exhaust, my body knew what was coming, and it responded. I strapped on my helmet but kept my visor open, and backed up out of my spot; then I knocked it into first and blew out of the parking lot so fast I almost didn't make it around the corner. Wind filled my lungs like the bellows of a concertina, and I roared past a stop sign, onto the main road.

Rowe is a beautiful place to ride; it's way out there, and the roads are well paved and sparsely populated. The incline rolls up and down all the way to Shelburne Falls, and the curves are sumptuous. The view I didn't appreciate just then, but the curves I hugged as tightly as if we were dancing. I was going fast enough to feel the breeze pushing me back and forth across the road, but I went faster. I glanced down at the speedometer, idly wondering where courage ends and carelessness begins.

I knew I should turn around, should slow down, dig up some rational thoughts and a couple of brain cells, but in that moment, with that kind of ferocious exuberance fluttering underneath my right palm, I couldn't bring myself to let up and straighten my wrist. It was like playing chicken with someone I couldn't see. I got down to Charlemont, riding recklessly the whole way, and I pulled into the gas station to fill up. I hadn't decided yet how far I was going, or in which direction, but I knew I was going to go fast. I put down the kickstand and took my helmet off, hooking the open visor onto the end of the handlebar as I climbed off. On the other side of the pump, a potbellied golfer filled his gold SUV and gave me a long, curious look. For a split second I saw myself in the reflection of his car window: flaming hair wired with static electricity, dark smudges of mascara under both eyes, practically quivering with rage.

"That's a nice bike," he said after a minute.

"Thanks."

"Used to have one just like it," he said. "What year is that? 'Eighty-something?"

"'Eighty-six."

"Brings me back."

I nodded and went into the gas station, bought five dollars' of premium, and filled up my tank. He was still there when I finished, and his pump was still going. He kept trying to catch my eye, but I wasn't having any of it. I put on my helmet.

"Hey," he said as I started the bike, "ride safe."

I snapped my visor down, and, looking at him through the tinted plastic, I saw an expression on his face that I recognized. The puckered eyebrows and earnest eyes, an uncertain slant to his mouth, a face that conveyed both worry and helplessness. It was my mother's face, after a disturbing phone call from Phin, or when I announced I was dropping out of high school. The man lifted a hand as I rode away from the pump, and I saw him turn to watch me pull out of the parking lot.

I rode a little farther, but it was getting dark fast. I felt the pull of gravity and followed it, sinking back into the atmosphere, into reality. I headed back to the camp. On the way, it rained a little, just enough to slick the roads, and I slowed down. I remembered that *Escape Velocity* was never my game, that I had nothing to prove. I remembered that I had a choice. Maybe Phineas didn't have that, maybe the twists and turns of his brain dictated his actions, his beliefs, but I sensed a decision waiting to be made, and so I reached down deep and I made it. I recognized it—a decision I'd made before, one I'll make again. The decision to pause, to pull back. I let my thoughts settle, my blood cool; I flexed my fingers. Speed and direction aligned. I leaned back into the wind and felt the throb of the engine buzzing through the soles of my boots and into the pads of my feet. Vibrations crept up my legs and down my arms. I listened to the whistle of air past my helmet and the hiss of my tires on the wet asphalt, the taste of soggy summer night air and gasoline on my tongue. The road straightened out, and for a long moment my velocity was constant—perfectly fluid, as if I were gliding.

WHEN I GOT BACK, the parking lot was quiet and the tarp was tangled in the tall grass where I had left it. I switched off the engine and the silence seemed to expand, to take up room around my mouth and eyes and ears like a physical presence, shushing me with some kind of invisible pressure. I unlaced the chin strap of my helmet and set it on my lap. Air rushed against my face, sound found its way to my ears: crickets in the scrub, frogs at the edge of the pond, birds murmuring in the trees.

I got off the bike and spread the tarp out over it, then I tucked it in, each corner laced through a wheel spoke and back again. I found the rock that had rolled under a car and repositioned it on the seat of the bike, a little extra weight just in case those clouds hanging over Vermont moved in and brought a storm with them, and then I tucked my helmet into the crook of my arm. The hollow between my heart and my stomach still ached, but my head felt clearer. The pounding need to move had abated, and the raw fury of rejection that had fueled me sputtered and went out. I felt spent, as if I'd been awake for days. As if I'd been riding for days. I looked back at the Rebel, bundled up in her blue tarp like a newborn, and I thought of that man at the gas station in Charlemont. His expression, so familiar it startled me, and my own, in the reflection of his car: jaw rigid, eyelids tight and narrow, nostrils flared, breath slow and heavy and ragged—unhinged. I recognized that one, too. I drew a line in the gravel with the heel of my boot as I fished a pack of cigarettes out of my breast pocket; then I turned away from the Rebel and started walking.

5.

Entropy

Entropy can be quantified as the amount of disorder in a closed system, or the measure of unavailable energy. It is a quantity that illustrates the simple but irrefutable fact that in nature, order tends toward disorder and never the opposite. Concentrated energy disperses, chemical bonds erode, heat cools, cold warms. Entropy must either increase or stay constant, which is why it is sometimes referred to as *time's arrow*—by discovering how much entropy, or disorder, is present, one can make inferences about the timeline of events. This isn't a scientific quirk, or a complex formula. This is fundamental, intrinsic to how we interpret what we see.

Imagine, for a moment: a motorcycle is on its side, debris everywhere, a car splayed sideways across the road and white steam curling from beneath the hood. There are sirens, and shouting, and the smell of spilt gasoline and burnt rubber.

Now look again: double yellow line, smooth pavement, and a motorcyclist whizzing down the road, her passenger's head turned to admire the view—a car in the distance, a deer poised in the brush.

And again: a motorcyclist and her passenger on an otherwise empty road, no one ahead, no one behind, just fresh black asphalt and warm afternoon light.

It doesn't take a scientist to know which snapshot comes when, and it doesn't take a scientist to know that the opposite sequence, the motorcycle spontaneously rising from its side, regaining its fallen passenger and rider, unbending its handlebars, and restarting its engine—is impossible. Entropy is a one-way street; this knowledge is innate. No one needs to explain why spilled milk stays spilled, or why milk tends to spill in the first place, it's only whether one cries about it or not that warrants an aphorism.

WHEN PHINEAS HEADED WEST I was about to begin my first year of high school. I had always been very concerned that I would somehow be trapped in the small suction cup of a town where I grew up, as if I might put down roots by accident, and so I became intent on the idea of boarding school. As I was always impatient to be moving forward, growing up and getting on with being an adult, it seemed like the thing to do. I was adamant about this, impatient to expand my horizons. My parents never had a hope of convincing me otherwise. I imagined finding kindred spirits at boarding school, learning amazing new things, becoming cool, attractive, edgy. I was terrified of venturing into the unknown, but also thrilled and so, so ready—this was it, I remember thinking, the beginning of growing up, the end of being a child, what a thrill. My mother gave me the enormous steamer trunk she had taken to college in the sixties, and I painted the inside of it a bright, robin's-egg blue. I was so pleased when I finished. Brush in hand, I stepped back to admire my handiwork in the flickering fluorescence of my father's woodshop, newspapers under the edges and painter's tape around the lip, imagining it in my dorm room. I still have the trunk, but I keep it mostly shut— the blue seems too bright, too obvious. It is an overly optimistic shade.

I had already begun to sense a little darkness in my thoughts, depths that hadn't been there before. Eighth grade fluttered by on gray wings, but that particular period of apathy was easy to dismiss as a symptom of my location. I'd begun to despise life in my small town and at my even smaller school. It wasn't so much the smallness itself that made me cringe, it was the small-mindedness, the insularity of the people around me. I was sure there had to be somewhere better, but I had yet to understand that the bleak and hopeless wasteland I was entering wasn't the landscape of my surroundings. It was within.

Discovering this inexplicable sadness was like flipping over a mossy rock in the woods and seeing the fat grubs and centipedes unearthed, writhing as the light touches them, or discovering a false bottom in my soul, a dark and foreboding extension of who I had believed myself to be. I was instantly ashamed, as if this was wrong, was somehow my own fault, and so I pretended it wasn't there. This was easy at first—there was no one to tell the difference. Phineas was in the wind by then—lost, but not yet found. My parents were home, in their empty nest, a little more than an hour south from me. My mother, keeping busy at her school, teaching art to kindergarten through twelfth grade, organizing the yearbook and the art fair and the half a dozen other extracurricular activities she always seemed to be in charge of; my father, listening to audiobooks in his woodshop as he made jewelry boxes and tables and stools, sanding them smooth, then varnishing them until the wood grain glistened like living golden veins.

I had chosen between two boarding schools, one large, preppy, and prestigious, one small and alternative, with a working farm on its campus. I don't fully remember my reasoning behind choosing the smaller school, but the idea that Phineas would approve certainly crossed my mind, as his approval had yet to lose its currency with me. When I toured it I saw kids with neon hair and piercings, in frayed jeans and muck boots, playing Ultimate Frisbee, dreading one another's hair, sketching on big pads with sticks of charcoal. The tour guide showed us the barn, with its rows of cows and a few students shaking containers full of feed, and the pond, where kids swam in their underwear. It was familiar, and at the same time it was a whole new universe. I could see myself there. At the other school they showed us the massive, silent library and a Vespers rehearsal, brick dorms, and pristine soccer fields. It was a beautiful campus, and utterly predictable. The first school drew me in with its strangeness. It magnetized me.

From the moment orientation began, there was so much to do, so little time to think, that I was carried through the first few months of my freshman year simply by the momentum of everyone around me. Yet this in and of itself began to eat away at me. Yes, my peers were interesting and unique, artists and farmers and activists and nerds, but I couldn't escape them, even for a moment. I had grown up with hours and hours to myself, whole days for sitting in the tall grass outside or reading in my room, and suddenly it wasn't possible to be alone. Suddenly, I needed to be in class, or at an activity, or at my work-study job, or doing homework, or socializing. I was almost immediately exhausted.

There was no time to address the sadness that was overtaking me, no way to release it. I upped the wattage of my smile to compensate, but it only made my energy fade faster. It only made me feel like a liar. Pretty soon I started acting like one, too. I lied about skipping classes, about smoking pot in the woods; I lied about the bottles of booze that I grew skilled at stealing; I lied about hallucinating with psilocybin mushrooms and unadvised amounts of cough-and-cold medication, watching the ceiling bubble and the walls breathe. All this was a way of searching for a release valve, some way to let just a breath of despair escape my body, because if I couldn't find relief I was sure I would burst.

Of the blur that was my freshman year, I remember most vividly the crowded crush of Milk Lunch, a mid-morning snack that the school served in the foyer of the dining hall. There was watery hot cocoa and cider and coffee and warm, gooey muffins laid out on a barricade of folding tables, plus a few hundred kids packed into the cramped space, waiting and pushing and squawking like a flock of gulls, crumbs falling from their mouths, muffin wrappers scattered across the floor. I remember entering the throng and feeling as though my head would explode, wishing fervently to disappear, to find myself somewhere, anywhere, else. Come to think of it, I felt like my head was about to explode for almost the entire year. I had always been a relatively easygoing kid—I didn't know what to make of the anxious, icy sweat trickling down my neck and behind my knees, didn't have the vocabulary or the knowledge or the perspective to understand what was happening to me.

Navigating boarding school as a naïve fourteen-year-old with depression and anxiety nipping at my heels was over-whelming, but when Phineas resurfaced at the end of that first semester, it became torture. All I wanted was to be liked, to make some friends, to not be ridiculed or flunk French, but even those modest goals felt insurmountable. I was sinking on my own, but then losing my brother took me straight to the bottom. First he sent me a box, full of his favorite things: T-shirts, CDs, books—no note, just things. Things I had always coveted—suddenly, I didn't want them anymore. We hadn't heard from him in months and I had no idea what this gift meant, but I went ahead and thought the worst. My parents reported a disturbing and irrational phone call from him, and then, after I sent a pleading letter to an address I had for him in Utah, begging him to come home, his sermons began to arrive. I kept them because they were so cruel. I knew I would second-guess myself later, that I would have to go back and reaffirm that he had indeed written that in bold, black ink. Seeing someone else's beliefs, someone else's words, in my brother's handwriting shook me, unsettled me like I had never been unsettled before. Someone else's words, but undoubtedly his own voice, his own twisted humor and slang and biting logic that I had always trusted implicitly as a child, even when he told me things like my new toy shark would expand and come alive if used in water; or watching *The Wizard of Oz* too many times would make me go blind; or cigarettes tasted like chocolate.

This time I was older, he was meaner, and I'd already been fooled one too many times. So when he wrote, *"You are a wretched excuse for a human, but you can have forgiveness from God. That is, if you so choose, or should I say, if God so chooses you,"* I had enough of a spine not to get down on my face and repent for my selfish little soul, as he suggested on page 11, but not enough to discard the claim that I was a wretched excuse for a human being. I was already so miserable it fit right in with the rest of my convictions. I internalized the brimstone, declined the salvation.

I don't recall many details from that year, though, oddly, I do remember seeking out old prom and bridesmaid dresses at secondhand stores and wearing them with black combat boots, underneath raggedy sweatshirts. I mention the dresses because I can picture them more clearly than the faces of most of my classmates. Something about the colors made me feel better—there was a lavender off-the-shoulder dress, mid-length, with a ribbed corset; a strapless iridescent blue ball gown, layer upon layer of shimmering fabric for a skirt, like shiny flower petals, and a purple silk lining; a spring-green frock with yellow roses embroidered on the collar. I changed my hair a lot—dying it one color, then another; cutting it short, letting it grow, cutting it even shorter, but I could never seem to look in the mirror without wanting to disappear. I kissed a boy for the first time, then a girl, or maybe the other way around, I can't remember for sure which came first. My mind was expanding so quickly, changing so rapidly, that the moment I thought I knew who I was everything would shift and I would lose track.

Summer arrived, and that helped. School let out, and gradually I could breathe again. I went back to my childhood home in southern Vermont, where the closest neighbor was a dairy farm a mile away and there were acres and acres of meadow or forest to wander in. The press of scheduled time and crowded assemblies ceased while my imagination took over, led me away from the harsh realities that had been bringing me low. But when my sophomore year rolled around it was like being dropped back into a barrel of ice water—constricting, cold, dark, and familiar in the worst way. The correspondence from my brother had lost its temporary, what-the-fuck-is-happening quality and become an old, stale pain that I still didn't understand. I started to realize that I never would, and that's probably around the time that the self-destruction I found myself experimenting with—binge drinking, popping pills, snorting them, putting cigarettes out on my arm, cutting myself with a razor blade—became difficult to conceal. All the rage I felt at being abandoned by Phineas, at the horrible hopelessness I couldn't help but attribute to him, was pointed inward.

In the end, everything I had been trying so desperately to hide became illuminated by an inquisitive spotlight. The dean found out and called my parents, who came and got me. I felt disgusted with myself and simultaneously not sorry at all. I had short-circuited, and there was the burnt-out fuse for everyone to see. There was pain in this shift, but also a strange, smoldering nugget of pleasure—a downward spiral was what came next in the blueprints Phineas had left me, a black hole, and in that respect, at least, I was on the right track. I dropped out around Thanksgiving, then enrolled in community college the next semester, acquiring credits that went toward appeasing my understandably freaked-out parents and also counted toward my high school requirements. From having two reasonably well-adjusted children, they had gone to one, and then to none. I didn't know what to tell them, how to explain something I didn't understand, either.

At this point, I can tell you how boarding school felt, but not how it was; can recall the colors I wore, but little about the roommates I lived with. The years after are a bit clearer. Post–boarding school, the psychology of mental illness became a fixation. I began to look for it in myself, in my own behavior and thought patterns. The chronic-depression diagnosis I received didn't interest me—hopelessness wasn't an answer, just another word for my day-to-day. Instead, I was captivated by delusions, hallucinations, paranoia, and breaks with reality, and I did all sorts of research in my spare time. I wished for this sort of disconnect in some small way—for the ability to do what Phin had apparently done, to disappear from the world entirely. To manufacture my own reality, then live there, forever. It was a precipice I played at the edge of a little too often and a little too eagerly.

Over the course of the next year my best friends were drugs and alcohol. I discovered sex, first with girls my own age, then with an assortment of men too old for me. At sixteen I got a car—a revelation. A game-changer. I could go where I liked when I liked, and the intoxication of this freedom thrilled me so deeply I came to crave speed and uncertainty whenever I stood still. The knowledge that I could take my keys and go, anywhere, and no one would be able to find me was exhilarating. When it came time to begin thinking about what to do next, all I knew was I would follow that exhilaration anywhere. My associate's degree quickly arrived on the horizon—I took classes during both the summer and winter breaks in order to finish sooner—and I began planning my disappearing act.

The flexibility of community college and the isolation of my childhood home set me at ease. I wasn't happy, but I was functional. I took night classes, worked breakfast shifts at local inns and B&Bs, and when I wasn't working or at school I was usually alone in Vermont, walking in the woods, reading or scribbling in my cramped loft. The loft had been my brother's room when we both lived in that house, and my room was below, but when he left I migrated upward. It was smaller than the lower room, the sloped ceiling barely high enough to stand up under, even at its peak and even for me. Its size never bothered either of us: there was a skylight, good for smoking out of, and the room was accessible only by ladder. A teenager's paradise. As I waited tables, cleaned hotel rooms, and cared for a five-year-old while I took night classes, I saved everything I earned in a wooden box next to my bed. Once a week or so I would take my five-year-old charge to the library to stock up on movies and picture books, and after we'd drive to the bank, where I would ceremoniously deposit a wad of assorted bills. The balance was rising ever so slowly, but the county was paying for my college classes and my parents were housing and feeding me—it had nowhere to go but up.

By the time I'd saved about two grand I was almost finished with my final semester at the Community College of Vermont. My last credits were from an intensive winter class, an online course, as I recall, so there was little to no fanfare over finishing. I certainly didn't mind—education had left an unpleasant taste in my mouth. I was burnt out from a perpetual roster of classes (though that was my own doing) and from the disaster that had been boarding school, feeling more than ready to leave standardized tests and textbooks behind. I can't even remember being congratulated, though of course I'm sure I was. I'd long since left the country by the time graduation rolled around, was already in Kilkee, Ireland, soaking my feet in the horseshoe bay, and didn't even see my diploma until four years after I'd earned it.

THE SAFETY CATCH between order and disorder is as natural to us as time's arrow. Mountains don't spontaneously fall down, even though that is the tendency of energy—they erode ever so slowly, and only as the cosmic glue that binds rock to rock disintegrates. Air-conditioned rooms stay cold because walls keep out the heat, just as heated rooms stay warm because walls keep out the chill, quarters and dimes abide the confines of a pocket, and when you plug a drain the sink fills with water. The presence of containers and confinements such as these is ridiculous to even describe—it goes without saying. It is only in their absence or failure that the pull toward disorder becomes palpable. An open door, a hole in your pocket.

By the time I turned seventeen, many of the boundaries that tend to contain seventeen-year-olds had already collapsed. I was done with college for the time being, and I was done with Vermont. I needed to break away from my parents, from my adolescence, from everything that had happened with Phineas, but there was nothing new to become attached to. My ambitions had all melted away, and so I was propelled forward not by a presence but by an absence. I didn't care about continuing my education, or beginning a career, or even having a good time. There was no one I felt connected to, no bond to anchor me. I drifted—not because I was moving toward anything but because there was nothing to keep me still.

JUST BEFORE I flew to Ireland, I took a walk during a blizzard along the dirt road that I grew up on, and all I could see were the fat, white snowflakes clinging to my eyelashes. I was taking my backpack, loaded to the gills, on a trial run before I went abroad, and in the spirit of testing my gear I was also wearing the yellow poncho I had purchased in anticipation of Ireland's rain, though perhaps my winter coat might have been the better choice. I wore a new pair of Red Wing boots, made of oxblood leather, tied with brown laces, that slowly softened into the shape of my feet as I walked. The bright yellow halo of the poncho's hood, like a circular picture frame, edged my vision, but it was all I could see. The rest was white.

Three orphaned kittens who were living in our woodshed trailed behind me as I trudged along, a little band of misfits that had gotten into the habit of following me around. Already the snow had overwhelmed their legs and was pressing up against their warm bellies. There were no tire tracks in front of us, no footsteps, no trees or power lines anymore, just thick, white powder covering everything and a dim, dirty-white sky.

When I turned and squinted to check on the kittens I saw only two, so I went back to scoop up the third, a smudge of orange fur drowning in white a ways behind the others, and tucked him inside my yellow jacket, where he purred steadily against my chest. The other two kittens eventually stopped and turned around, but the orange tom and I kept going—he kept purring, I kept walking, the blizzard kept coming, and together we disappeared into its blank, white stare.

Several weeks later I boarded a plane in Boston amid more snow, the Red Wings on my feet, the backpack in cargo, and crossed the ocean. Disembarking in Ireland, I began a journey that would last longer and extend farther than I'd ever expected. Along my way, I would learn that the kittens who had followed me so faithfully into that blizzard disappeared the same month I did. I comforted myself by imagining them finding adventure—a new life in a strange place, just like me. It may be unlikely that a trio of kittens could survive a forest full of predators and emerge on the other side, but I don't think it's impossible. Survival is easy. It's living that's hard.

6.

Friction

The summer I bought the Rebel I went to a local dealership to get it inspected. It was before I left to work at the camp in Rowe, an hour north of my house in Northampton. In the service area there was a makeshift office, nestled among the oil stains and the scattered tools, fitted with a desk, a watercooler, and two screechy rolling chairs. Roy, the proprietor, sat in one, me in the other. I watched as he riffled through a mound of paperwork on his desk, leaf by leaf, throwing nearly all of it into the waste bin, and I waited. Finally, he looked at me and asked, for the second time, what I wanted.

"An inspection," I repeated. He fell silent, threw away a few more things, and let the pause go on so long I wondered if maybe he'd forgotten I was there. Again.

"Bring your bike up to the line," he grumbled eventually.

"Actually, it's that one," I said, and I pointed to it, parked with the front tire on the white line, just like he'd asked, not ten feet from where we were sitting. He made an unhappy little noise in his throat, as though being bullied, as though he'd rather not be wasting his time with this girlish intruder. The other, younger mechanic, who had been making eyes at me since I walked in, snorted under his breath; it occurred to me that I didn't know which one of us he was laughing at, but I suspected either way the joke was on me.

Finally, Roy stood, pulling himself up by the edge of the desk. The chair rolled away from him as he got to his feet and chirped to a halt near a glowing yellow Chopper parked next to the open door. He shuffled over to my bike, which looked tiny beside the hulking monsters that crowded the edges of the shop, took a little ruler out of his shirt pocket, and started measuring the tread on my tires. He told me I'd need to replace them soon, but that he'd let it go for now.

"Cute little bike you got here," he said with a condescending smile. "At least it starts with the right letter." The right letter is *H*, and according to men like Roy, of whom I've met many, the right ending is *ARLEY*, letters that spell not only an all-American motorcycle manufacturer but an all-American lifestyle. I made what I hoped was a polite but discouraging sound—squabbling over one's preferred make of motorcycle is infantile. Either it runs or it doesn't; either you ride it or you don't. If you want to ride a Harley, then buy one. If you want *everyone* to ride a Harley, then move to Daytona or shut the fuck up about it.

His huge midsection flared out from his slight frame like a ballerina's tutu, precariously balanced on his slender legs and tiny, tennis-shoed feet as he moved around the bike, inspecting. He crouched down to check my oil, then my front axle. Leaning in close, he poked the front brake pads with a pen.

"You're in trouble over here," he said, and stood up slowly. "You need new brake pads." He paused and chewed on his pen for a minute, then reasoned, "But you probably don't know what those are." I ground my teeth together with a squeak that made my head ache. The younger mechanic snorted again and looked over at us. I glared at him, and he went back to his carburetor.

"I know what brake pads are," I snapped, but Roy wasn't listening anymore, he was lumbering back over to the makeshift office.

He retrieved his chair from near the Chopper on his way and rolled it back over to the desk. When he sat down, the scream of creaking metal was so shrill I thought the springs might snap, but they held admirably. He shuffled through some more papers. I stayed by the bike. To soothe myself, I imagined knocking over that entire flock of motorcycles, like shining, flawless dominoes crashing down, one after another. They would topple, starting with the Chopper, until they had all crumpled into one long, metallic mountain ridge. I imagined the silence that would follow, the eerie moment of an echo, then the final crunch of a mirror splintering.

"I'm gonna pass you this time," he said finally, like it was against his better judgment, "but get those tires replaced and don't forget about your front brakes. You want a quote?"

"No, I can do it myself," I lied. I would figure it out eventually; maybe Rigdhen could give me some pointers.

Chuckling, Roy ripped off a receipt for the inspection from his pad and handed it to me. "If that don't work out, you feel free to come back. I'll give you a good deal."

I said thanks as gracefully as I could manage, not very, forked over fifteen dollars, and hit the pavement. The sun was out, I had the day off, and it was only the beginning of my first motorcycling season. I let my arms hang slack from the handlebars and my shoulders relax, then I opened up the throttle, knocked the Rebel up a gear, and let her do the rest.

NOTHING STRENGTHENS determination quite like skepticism. The idea to replace my own brake pads was born the moment Roy insinuated that I couldn't do it, and it was the same when I'd decided to go abroad as a teenager: the friendly and familial doubt that met my initial airing of the idea only made me more certain that I would do it. The particular friction of someone else's disbelief or doubt, that chafing between what I think I can do and what someone else thinks I can do, is as infuriating as it is irresistible.

In the physical world, *friction* is defined as the force that resists relative motion between two surfaces—the quantity of resistance. It isn't a straightforward force, like a push or a pull, nor is it constant in its application like gravity; it's unpredictable, with a whole host of variations. There's fluid friction, internal friction, lubricated friction, dry friction, and the list goes on. Dry friction comes to mind first, simply specifying that the two objects or surfaces coming into contact with each other are solid. Within dry friction, there are two subcategories: static and kinetic. Static friction occurs between two objects that are not moving relative to each other. A motorcycle parked on an incline is relying on static friction to stay stationary, but if that same motorcycle were being ridden down the freeway, it would still be relying on the static friction between the pavement and the tire to stay in control. The bike is moving, the wheels are spinning, but as each inch of rubber connects with another inch of highway, in that moment those two surfaces rely on static friction to keep them joined. Lay some ice down on the road and it's a different story—it's kinetic friction.

Kinetic friction occurs when two objects or surfaces are moving relative to each other. The element of ice undoes the static friction the motorcycle tires were relying on from the road, and suddenly those tires are slipping all over the place—but what has changed? A new surface has been introduced to the mix, ice rather than concrete, and along with this comes a new frictional coefficient. The *coefficient of friction* is a number that describes the ratio between the force necessary to move an object or surface against another and the pressure between the two surfaces. For example, the frictional coefficient for rubber on dry concrete is 1.0. For rubber on wet concrete it's 0.7. Rubber and ice? 0.15. These numbers don't come from calculations, they are empirical measurements, which means that they come from experimentation and observation. There is no formula for friction.

It was a week or two after the inspection. I was at the youth camp in Rowe, warming up to my affair with motorcycles. I stood up from examining the front wheel, and my knees left sandy dimples in the road. Dusting off my hands and my gravel-studded shins, I considered the scant handful of teenagers that crowded around the Rebel. The Clymer maintenance, troubleshooting, and repair manual for this model lay facedown on the black seat, open to the chapter on brakes—front brakes, rear brakes, brake maintenance, brake pads, brake rotors, brake troubleshooting: we were hot and thirsty and totally stumped.

That afternoon we had wandered down to the parking lot with our chests puffed out and our elbows cocked, looking to start a project. We had brought my dusty toolbox, filled with tools swiped from an abandoned garage and a brand-new ratchet set on loan from a friend, the Clymer manual, a bag of salted pretzel rods, and some shiny new brake pads, still in the package. The ruse was that this was a summer camp activity, that I knew what I was doing, and that I was going to teach them something.

I explained to them the basics of how to ride, even though they weren't quite old enough, how the brakes worked, what we were aiming to do, and then we sat in the dirt and tried to figure out how to do it. I had already read the chapter, but being handy is something I only aspire to—I have never had that instinctive knowledge of how things work the way someone like my father does. Sometimes I can see the gears clicking together in his eyes when he looks at a machine, or the boards joining up when he looks at a house, and his hands just know where to go, what to do, what's wrong and how to fix it. It's miraculous; but for me, that base intuition into how something *works* just isn't there. I see what it does, how to use it, but the inner life of objects has never been visible to me like that.

The teenagers and I tinkered on, eating pretzels, showing off, flipping through the manual. The sand we sat on got hot, and then the metal on the bike got hotter, and then we hit a wall. We couldn't apply enough force to a small, awkwardly positioned place on the front brake caliper in order to make room for the new brake pads.

Braking on any vehicle is essentially the transference of a small force created by the driver, in this case the pressure on the lever of the right handlebar, into a larger force that slows the rotation of the wheel by maximizing the friction between the brake pads and the rotor. On a motorcycle, when you squeeze the front brake, it compresses the brake fluid that flows through the brake line to the caliper on the front wheel. Pinned to the caliper and clamped onto the disk rotor are the brake pads, two little pancake pieces of metal that catch the rotor between their graphite palms every time the rider brakes and slow its rotation. The two pads are pressed together by the force provided from the compressed brake fluid, which has nowhere else to go, so it extends the caliper pistons, which compress the brake pads, which make contact with the rotor and create the friction that slows the vehicle. The brake pads slowly wear away with each use; the heat of the friction, the grind against the disk rotor—it all takes its toll, and if you let them wear too thin you run the risk of grinding through the rotor. The problem might start as a soft squeal or a squeak, but eventually you will lose the ability to brake effectively.

We had gotten the caliper off the wheel and the old brake pads out without too much trouble, but the problem that the afternoon inevitably presented wasn't covered in the Clymer manual, and, like I said, we were stumped. As the brake pads wear down, they become thinner, and as they become thinner the brake fluid level adjusts to keep them firmly pinned to the rotor by the caliper pistons. On the Rebel, the pistons had seized in an extended position and the new brake pads, fat and fresh as they were, couldn't fit into the space. We had tried to force the pistons back, to no avail. Even our strongest efforts yielded disappointing results.

There is a level of raw strength that is required in auto mechanics—to loosen a bolt that hasn't moved in decades, or to fit a part into a space that will barely accommodate it— but there is also a certain tenderness that is called for. You wouldn't drag a big piece of furniture across a polished hardwood floor, the friction would scuff the hell out of it; you find a way to move it without damaging the wood. It's the same working on motorcycles—no unconstructive friction. Find another way.

The pistons were impossible, and even though we were trying to be careful, there were a few shallow scratches on the caliper that hadn't been there before: never a good thing. The workshop slot ended and the teenagers drifted away, thrilled by the smell of grease, unfazed, I hoped, by the failure. I stubbed the dirt with my toe and watched them disperse. There had to be another way to go about it.

If the essential concept behind motorcycle brakes is to transfer a small force in the front brake lever into a larger force in order to compress the brake pads, then that conversion of force also works the other way around. After the campers left that afternoon, I went hunting for a clamp— something that wouldn't slip the way the crowbars and wooden wedges we had been trying did, and could exert a large amount of force transferred through a measured, relatively small force applied by me. I eventually found one with a little help, and in the near dark I sat cross-legged in the sandy parking lot and fastened the clamp onto the extended pistons. I tightened it, and as I wound the crank, the pistons sank back into the caliper. I slotted in the new brake pads and fished the unfastened pins out of a canning jar I kept in my toolbox for loose parts. I attached the caliper to the rotor, pumped the brakes a few times to tighten the fluid and test the friction, then I sat down with my back against the car parked next to my bike.

Almost as soon as I started riding motorcycles, I became eager to learn how they worked. Roy wasn't my first encounter with mockery surrounding my new interest, and he wasn't my last. While reactions like his inspired my irritation, they also fueled me with a thirst for mechanics. It made me realize that my capability as a motorcyclist was going to be constantly called into question and that I'd better do my homework: at the very least, learn to name the components of my vehicle, their function, how they fit together. There's an elegant simplicity to motorcycles, especially old ones—the engine is right there, the mechanisms exposed. I may not be able to *fix* it, but the least I can do is figure out how it works. This stuff isn't easy for me, but I owe it to myself to learn what I can, whether it comes fast or slow, easy or hard.

I leaned my head back on the driver's-side door and found an early star in the dusty blue sky—just one, though—and I nudged my toolbox shut with my foot. The snap of the latch echoed, bouncing between the cars and the softly murmuring maple trees. I fished a wrench out of the sand that I almost hadn't seen and I turned it over in my hands. I balanced it on my palm, testing the weight of it, then I opened the box and laid it down among the other tools.

7.

Gravity

During that same summer there was a party at my house in Northampton. At the northern tip of the Knowledge Corridor, and in the midst of the Five College area, Northampton teems with young people; there was no shortage of parties there, either at that house or in Northampton, but this one I remember in particular. We barbecued ribs and dogs and burgers in our backyard all afternoon, and sometime around dusk it seemed as though the entire neighborhood was there. The gathering began in the small, overgrown backyard, but by the evening it was spilling down the driveway and into the road.

We had speakers pointed out through the open living room windows, playing Merle Haggard and Dolly Parton and assorted prog rock on vinyl, someone running inside to flip the record every twenty minutes, and there was a table literally covered with bowls of salad: pasta salad, egg salad, potato

salad, spinach salad, rice salad, arugula salad. There was a
bowl of M&M's being called a sugar salad. Someone's dog
lapped melted ice out of a plastic bucket full of Pabst Blue
Ribbon sitting next to the porch. I heard it growl when a
young man reached in for a can of beer, and the young man
growled back.

I watched as a steady stream shuffled in and out the back
door of my house, to and from the grill, carrying paper plates
that buckled under mounds of food, plastic forks rising up out
of the middles like flagpoles. They found spots on the grass,
among the forgotten croquet wickets, and they dug in, emerging with barbecue sauce on their cheeks and under their
fingernails, corn in their teeth, and red wine stains on their
lips. Someone slapped a round of tofu dogs on the squat, brick
grill in the center of it all, and another swarm of guests arrived, bringing with them a chorus of carbonation, that sharp
snap-fizz of half a dozen aluminum cans being cracked open
at once.

The Rebel was parked where I could see it, just at the edge
of the lawn, with the front tire on the grass. I sat on the porch
railing, my feet hooked into the rungs, admiring the day and
eating a handful of sugar snap peas while I talked to Chuck
Meyer about motorcycles he'd ridden as a young man. Chuck
was the father of my good friends. His daughter was roughly
my age, but his two sons were nearer to my brother's. In fact,
Phin had been close with Chuck's sons—there was even a
summer that he'd practically lived at their house in Conway.

As a teenager, I had clung to my brother's friends—Chuck's sons and a handful of others—as if by becoming part of their group I could keep him in some way. Though I'd lost touch with all of them while I'd been abroad, when I returned they were still there, playing noise music or making weird art, wearing T-shirts as thin and frayed as spiderwebs, shaving rarely, swimming often, working just enough to buy food and beer, exactly how I remembered. It soothed me to see them thriving: growing older with their ideals, staying constant in so many ways but also becoming more fully realized. We still gathered at Chuck's house in Conway on hot summer nights, and as time wore on and we all got a little older, Chuck became more and more likely to join us.

Although Chuck had been remembering my name at his kids' parties in the year since I'd returned to the area, it was my brother he'd known first. I am magnetized by the fossils of my brother's youth, of the "before," an attraction that has become so familiar I barely notice it anymore. Perhaps this is the foundation on which my friendship with Chuck was built. It might be the foundation for more than I care to admit.

I think one of the first things I remember learning about Chuck was his steady consumption of periodicals: *The Advocate*, *The Recorder*, *The New York Times*, *The Sun*, *The New Yorker*, *Harper's*—anything you could subscribe to, really, it seemed he had a subscription to. I remember coveting the stacks of glossy magazines, full of current events and literature, piled all over his house, trying to read as many as I could whenever

I visited, as if by flipping each page I would absorb the same worldly wisdom that settled on Chuck like dust.

He had been a newspaperman in his youth, some hotshot editor in New York or Long Island or maybe both, which accounts for his dedication to the written word, but for as long as I'd known him Chuck had been living in rural Massachusetts as a freelance pilot. He had a small aerial photography business consisting of a little plane parked out in Shelburne Falls, and he flew as much as he could. The sky seemed to occupy his thoughts almost as relentlessly as the words he so carefully spoke and so avidly read.

At that point I already knew about the Honda CM450 parked in Chuck's garage. Earlier in the summer, before I found the Rebel, I had suggested buying it from him, but he had shied away from the idea—had said he wanted to ride it again someday, but that I could borrow it whenever I wanted to, as long as I promised not to break my neck. It was quite an offer, but then the Rebel materialized; I fell hard for that electric-blue paint job and bought it without thinking twice.

I passed Chuck a sugar snap and he mentioned getting the CM on the road again. He hadn't ridden it in years. "She was running okay when I put her to bed," he said, and turned to admire the Rebel with me. He strode up to it and swung a leg over. I hopped down from my perch and followed him. Chuck got comfortable in the seat, rocked the bike back and forth a little, tested the shocks, squeezed the brakes. "If I had long pants on," he said, looking wistfully down at his bare legs, "I'd take her for a spin." He smiled then, and for a minute I couldn't tell if he was serious, if he was really game to zoom off down the road if only he were wearing pants. At times, the jokes he cracked were delivered with such an elegant deadpan I didn't even suspect I was hearing a joke until after he hit me with the punch line and was waiting for me to get it, nonchalantly fluffing that newspaper he always seemed to have in his hands, trying to hide a crooked, roguish grin in the folds of the Arts section.

The idea of Chuck taking a spin, with long pants or without, made me smile, but somehow I knew he wasn't joking just then. He had a thick head of downy white hair, carefully parted on the side, and a trim, lightly peppered, heavily salted beard. He was tall, a little stooped, as though he'd lost a few inches over the years, and he had a limp, but nevertheless he was a force. It wasn't possible for Chuck Meyer to enter a room unnoticed. "Next time I'll bring the long pants," he added solemnly, in the carefully enunciated, almost Mid-Atlantic accent that I've heard lovingly impersonated so many times. Since he had his shorts on, I could see the leg brace that was usually tucked away under his pants, and it gave him an endearing, lopsided look.

Chuck put the kickstand up on the Rebel and centered its weight. For a moment, he didn't say anything, he just leaned back a little, his right hand resting on the throttle, and squinted straight ahead like he had the wind in his face. Maybe he was looking at his son Nick, tending the tofu dogs on the grill, or his daughter, Anna, eating coleslaw and laughing so hard she couldn't swallow; maybe he was remembering a ride he'd taken as a young man—or something else altogether. He nudged the kickstand back down and got off the bike.

"Fantastic," he said. "I remember now."

A little while later he got the CM fixed up. A handyman friend went over to help him out with the mechanics. They filled the tank, jumped the battery, changed the oil, and started her up. Chuck gave me a call sometime in September.

"Hey, motorcycle buddy, how about a motorcycle ride," he said, and we picked a day when the weather looked good— he was always on the lookout for clear skies.

I rode out to his house in Conway on a Sunday morning, about twenty miles north. It was early and sunny and cold, and even though I had long johns on, the wind blew right through me. My feet were frozen chunks of flesh, knocking the gears up and down by memory because I couldn't feel what I was doing. I remember my hands burning from the cold and my teeth locked together to keep from chattering, and then, suddenly, a long stretch of road in the full sun. I flexed my fingers and felt the warmth soften the clamp of my jaw, part the clench of my teeth. I put it in fifth, and this time I could feel my toes knocking the gear up a notch. The air in my helmet got warmer. The thick hide of my jacket began to toast under the rallying sun, its beams like honey on my wind-chafed knuckles and my battered, bare throat. I let it soak in.

When I got there, Tchotchke, Chuck's lumbering black beast of a dog, lurched out of the house to greet me. Chuck followed. Tchotchke was a moody son of a bitch—he'd been known to snap if you touched him wrong, but as far as Chuck was concerned, he was putty. It was just the two of them out there, in that sprawling house, and I imagined them roaming the floor plan together, navigating the furniture, inspecting the rooms, securing the perimeter. Chuck had been divorced for years, and although lady friends had come and gone, he had been a bachelor for as long as I'd known him. It was just Chuck and Tchotch out there in Conway, and that was how I often thought of them—as a pair, the master and his minion, grizzled but noble; grumpy, alert, and stubborn as hell.

Chuck gave me a big hug and then a slap on the back. Tchotchke grumbled, good-naturedly, I hoped, and loped over to sniff my motorcycle. From behind, he was more bear than dog. I went inside to pee, borrow a pair of gloves, stomp my feet a little. I paused at the kitchen counter while I was inside, and I saw one of Chuck's to-do lists. There was always a to-do list lying around at Chuck's house, written out in one continual line, like this:

MILK TOMATO COTTAGE CHEESE MUSTARD
~~RECYCLING~~ OIL CHANGE DISH DETERGENT

BATTERIES PAPER TOWELS ~~GO TO DMV~~ BUY
TICKETS CALL RON SCHEDULE PHYSICAL
~~SHAMPOO~~

He would use the same sheet of paper until it was full. *Milk* would be written and crossed out five or more times, and the ink along the creases would be faint by the time he was ready to throw it out. Before we left, he went through another list, this one in his head, as if he were readying his plane for takeoff. He was crossing things off, one by one, in the dust on his gas tank. Fuel line, on; key, on; power switch, on; gear, neutral; clutch, in. My bike was still warm, but we sat and let his run with the choke out for a minute. Tchotchke watched us, his head cocked. On cold days, or when the bike hasn't been turned on in a while, pulling out the choke lessens the airflow and increases the ratio of gas entering your engine. More gas burns quicker in a cold engine, but enriching the mixture can also strip off the oil you need for lubrication, not to mention it uses up a lot of gas, so it's not sustainable— it's useful only if the bike won't start otherwise. He turned the choke off after a minute and gave me a thumbs-up. I motioned for him to go in front. He revved the throttle, got his feet off the ground and the bike into second gear after a little wobbling between the frostbitten ruts in the dirt road, and then were off. The day felt warmer, the sun higher. We tooled down through Conway's twists and turns, into Shelburne Falls, then we rode along Route 2, a meandering east-west highway that runs across the entire state of Massachusetts, but which is relatively sluggish and scenic as it passes through Franklin County.

We stopped at Gould's Sugarhouse, having already planned to meet Chuck's daughter, Anna, and her mom, Florence, there for brunch. We ate french toast and eggs, and I almost couldn't believe how nice it was to be sitting there with the three of them. Anna whispered that she thought my bike was cooler than Chuck's, and he scowled good-naturedly. After we ate, Anna and Florence waved us off, and Chuck and I kept going toward Greenfield. I remember pulling out of the parking lot after him, seeing him drag his feet a little too long, switch gears a little too abruptly, a little too soon, and I grinned to myself, thinking that even if we went thirty miles per hour all afternoon, it was the kind of perfect day you might hope and hope for but almost never get. I let it soak in.

WE SNUCK IN a few more weekend rides before the season ended and it was time to put the bikes to bed. At that point in my life, Sundays were sacred. I was in the midst of my first semester back in school since going to community college, when I was mostly concerned with doing the bare minimum, and a lot had changed since then. I was keenly aware of the debt I was accruing, and I was wholly invested in every single one of my classes. I wasn't totally sure what I wanted to study, just that I wanted to be a student again and I wanted to be good at it. I'd applied to one school, the University of Massachusetts, Amherst, because it was close and cheap, and once I sent in the application, the logistics fell into place. I enrolled over the summer, as a junior, and suddenly my rambling way of life—lazy mornings, work in the evenings, then drinking till dawn—shifted into a strenuously organized, deeply purposeful existence.

Sunday was the only day of the week that I didn't go to work or to campus or both, and I usually spent it curled up in bed, looking at my Kanji flashcards under the covers and catching up on all the bullshit that had fallen through the cracks during the week on my antiquated little laptop. As a rule, my feet didn't touch the floor until sometime in the late afternoon, when the e-mails had been sorted, the Japanese worksheets copied out, the physics equations scribbled on graph paper, and my legs had stopped aching from the Saturday-night rush, but those riding adventures with Chuck somehow managed to get me out of bed early. I looked forward to them as one of my only respites from an otherwise grueling routine.

ONE SUNDAY we went flying in his plane instead. I met him at the airport, grumpy and sleep-deprived. It was bright, so bright the sunglasses I was wearing didn't seem to be helping at all, then I remember looking up and realizing the sky was totally cloudless, a perfect day for flying. The mood lifted. I watched a bird riding the thermals and sighed, thinking, That will be me soon. I had found the airport without too much trouble, but when I got there, I wasn't so sure *airport* was the right word for it. I wandered through an open chain-link gate into a cluster of small airplane hangars set out in rows, each the same size and shape, and a road right down the middle. At first it seemed like I was alone, but as I walked farther in I saw a few planes being rolled out of their hangars, a few pilots and passengers loading up their gear, all of whom gave me a wave or a friendly nod. It reminded me of that brief gesture between motorcyclists: the recognition of someone else traveling among the elements, of someone else as close to the road as you are. I found Chuck eventually, getting the plane set up and checking everything over. He showed me where to put my bag, and then where to put myself. "Ready?" he asked. "Ready," I said. And after some more checking and double-checking, he got in and started her up.

I've flown a lot over the years; the view from high above the earth is nothing new to me, but flying with Chuck was different. It felt new. The wind shook our little plane, and we shouted at each other over the roar of the engine. My headset kept slipping off my head, and my feet tingled from the vibration of the floor. Cold air slipped in between the window-panes. The sky was so close I could have touched it.

We crossed the New Hampshire border and flew to Keene for lunch at an Indian restaurant—the only restaurant—in the airport. The airport itself was cold and empty, and mainly just a lobby with two restrooms and this little gray Indian place off to the side. The décor was surprisingly somber, like that of a nursing-home dining room, but the woman who took our order was awash with color, wearing a red-and-orange sari with gold borders and bangles and kohl around her eyes. Her bracelets clattered whenever she moved.

Chuck and I talked about flying and riding and the opera while we ate chicken makhani and saag aloo and watched the planes take off, like shaking little birds buffeted back and forth by the wind as they rose into the sky. We walked around the runway for a bit and then flew back to Massachusetts. Toward the end of the flight he told me to look out my window. "Seem familiar?" he shouted over the engine. I looked hard, trying to figure out what I was seeing, and then I realized it was Amherst, and there was my house, a tiny gray dot of shingles down among the fading foliage and the green-brown pastures. "I'll just drop you off here," he said and grinned. "Grab that parachute in the back and get ready to jump."

GRAVITY PRESENTS ITSELF to us most often as the force that gives weight to mass and causes objects to fall toward the ground, but in its essence it is a phenomenon that attracts matter to matter. It is the force behind the creation of the earth, of its orbit around the sun, and of the sun itself. The cosmic implications of gravity are both thrilling and overwhelming, though perhaps its earthly qualities are what we tend to think of first. The effects of gravity are so widespread, so all-consuming, that when the ancient Greeks began to think about motion, they couldn't see it—it was too big. From its manifestation in celestial mechanics down to keeping our shoes firmly pressed against the ground, gravity is a force to be reckoned with.

Newton said that the law of gravity dictates that mass is attracted to mass, with a force directly proportional to the product of the two masses and inversely proportional to the distance between them: the stronger the force of gravity, the larger the masses and the less distance between them.

THE LAST RIDE Chuck and I took that year was to the Ashfield Fall Festival, an annual Columbus Day weekend fair in rural Mass, a little west of Conway, with artisans, food, live music, dancing, and throngs of locals and tourists alike. My motorcycle was making an unsettling noise in high gears and I hadn't had the time to get it looked at, so we just took Chuck's. I rode on the back and admired the leaves as we puttered along the scenic route. The fair itself was quaint and crowded—we met Nick, one of Chuck's sons, and some other friends there. We scouted out the french fries at the fire station and then the cider doughnuts at Elmer's. At a fine woodworker's tent my friend Kieran called me over and showed me a wooden spoon with a challenge attached—*Guess what variety of wood this spoon is made of and win something*—I forget what the prize was. The vendor said that in more than ten years of fairs and festivals no one had guessed, although it's a tree everyone knows. "Only one guess," he said. "Them's the rules."

I thought back to my childhood; tried to imagine my father's workshop, the smell of sawdust, the stacks of sliced burls and planed boards. Curly maple, black walnut, ash, pine, cedar. I don't remember what I guessed, but the spoon kept its mystery.

On the ride back, we went the long way again. The leaves were at their best, the sunlight shining through their veined skin and dappling the road with muted color. We were going slow enough not to feel the bite of the wind, and the sun was high enough to keep us in its gaze. I remember everything— my feet on the pegs, Chuck's windbreaker under my fingers, the warmth of his back, the warmth of the afternoon and those colors: exploding all around us, burnished and gilded branches stretching out over the freshly turned road.

Somehow my memory of that day is crisper than my memory of yesterday. It's so strange the way a moment can crystallize that way, like a fly in amber—another mystery.

I SAW CHUCK a few times over the winter. On Thanksgiving Day I ate dinner at the long trestle table in his house. He presided over all those pies as the loving patriarch, and though he was a diabetic, I do believe he tasted every one. It was a good day; the house was full, the expensive whiskey was out and the fancy china, too. An inebriated relative got a little too flirtatious, and Chuck limped to my rescue, a gentleman to the end.

Over the holidays, I went out to Conway a few more times, and sometime after New Year's I set him up with a woman named Elizabeth I thought he'd like. I'd been meaning to see if he would be interested in the idea for ages, and then one night I went for it. I described her, and he was intrigued. "She looks like me at fifty," I said, because we have often been mistaken for mother and daughter—something to do with the color of our hair and the way we smile. "Well, then, I definitely want to meet her," he replied with a wink: pure Cary Grant. I gave him her number. That was the last time I saw him before he went to South America for a few weeks with Anna, a father-daughter adventure. After he got back, Chuck had some surgery on his leg and was laid up in Conway for a while. I heard, secondhand, that Chuck had called Elizabeth, that they'd gone on a few dates—but I hadn't gotten the scoop, not yet.

NOT LONG AFTER I heard all this, I got a phone call from Elizabeth. Something was wrong, that much I knew immediately. There was a blood clot, she said, and she stopped. I could hear her choking on tears in the silence that followed. I didn't need her to finish—I felt the weight settle on my shoulders and there was nothing to do but bear it, even know-ing that elsewhere the gravity of the situation would be tele-scoping spines and crushing sternums: the less distance there is, the stronger the force of gravity. The weight of loss is dif-ferent for everyone. What I thought had been our last ride of the year became our last ride altogether. I couldn't wrap my head around it. To accept the finality of death over the years that follow is one thing, but to understand it when it is right next to us—sometimes it's a truth we approximate, an idea too big to think about all at once.

I couldn't help but think of Phineas, and though death and absence are two very different things, it was the gravity of loss that connected them for me. I wondered how everything would have turned out if he had died or disappeared com-pletely instead of becoming someone else—if the gravity of that loss might have hurt more, or perhaps less. I wondered if my fourteen-year-old heart might have been better equipped to grieve for the dead than for the living.

A FEW DAYS AFTER Chuck's death, I went to his house in Conway, where his family, his children and grandchildren, and some of his friends gathered around the dining room table and shared the casseroles, the fruit plates and the cheese plates, the pies, stews, and cold cuts that had been accumulat-ing as the waves of sympathy crashed against the front door. Everyone said "I love you" more often than usual, and hugs turned into hanging on. I'm not the only stray that family has taken in over the years—Chuck's roof has housed more lost souls than I care to count, and so the mishmash of family and friends simmered, the line between them crisp and fuzzy all at once. An electric charge of grief ran through the floorboards, and the air was humid, heavy with salt water. We told stories and looked at photo albums, and I remember lingering over a list I found on the kitchen table. I counted *MILK* three times. The first two were crossed out, but the third was unmarked. There was an altar near the window, covered with old snapshots and little memories: a few feathers, an empty bottle of expensive whiskey, Chuck's reading glasses. The candles were lit, and reflections of the flames played across the glass panes behind them.

WHEN I REMEMBER CHUCK now I feel a sharp, quiet ache, and a warm glow. I think of something he said. We were on a dirt road framed by maples just beginning to turn—flakes of yellow and orange speckled the canopy above us, and the trees curled overhead like the vaulted ceiling of a cathedral. The road stretched out in front of us, and from where I stood it seemed infinite. The air was warm and humid, the dirt softly steaming after an unseasonably hot day, and between the trees I could see the sun settling down into the crook of the mountains, glowing red-hot as it sank, straight ahead from where we stood. I watched him as he picked up his helmet, strapped it on, and started his bike. I started mine, too; swung my leg over.

"I wish these things had wings," he shouted over the roar of the engine, then he got on and took off: down the road, toward the sun.

8.

Inertia

My second motorcycle wasn't much to look at. It wasn't much of anything, really. It didn't run, had no title, and although I briefly entertained the idea of fixing it up, the fact was I didn't have the skills or the money required. It quickly became an educational demolition project, one that only progressed about as far as the transmission before the gearbox seized and it was stranded outside for good.

I had just moved to a drafty old farmhouse in Amherst, on the other side of the Connecticut River, about a half hour northeast of Northampton, and I borrowed a pickup truck to relocate the motorcycle from its temporary home at Chuck's house in Conway. It was just before my first semester back at college when I went to collect it, six months or so before he died. A few musician friends leaving to go on a cross-country tour were staying there, and they helped me load the motorcycle into the back of the truck with a plywood ramp; then we waved each other off on our respective journeys. The truck was riding low from the extra weight, but it was still higher than I was used to. The motorcycle swayed against the straps as it peeked over the cab, parked at a jaunty diagonal angle, kickstand down, its disconnected headlight hanging from a single wire that knocked against the frame of the bike as I rumbled out of the driveway.

I watched in my rearview as the boys crammed one last amplifier into the trunk of the green Subaru that was about to become their home and swung out onto the dirt road. Dust came in through the open window and rocks jumped up to bite the thin flooring under my feet. I tilted the seat back a notch and dug around in the center console until I found a pair of shades, then hit Seek on the radio and let it flip through the stations for a minute, letting half-measures of pop songs slip past until at last I found some music without words. The wind, the gold ragweed pollen, and the dust from the road trickled in, settling on my skin like fine, sun-kissed silt. I tried to empty my head, to let my thoughts slip out the open window. I just followed the road, one eye on the motorcycle in my mirrors. It was good to be so high above the pavement for once. I surveyed, rather than participated in, the traffic, and when a gang of hogs rolled past me in South Deerfield, I lifted my arm from where it rested on the edge of the window in greeting. They sounded their horns at the sight of the motorcycle carcass I was towing in back and nodded solemnly to me as they roared past, as if we were all in on the same secret.

THE PLACE I HAD just moved to in Amherst was a big, butter-yellow farmhouse set close to the road, with a backyard that reached all the way to the woods. When I arrived in early September, it was a leafy paradise; there was a front porch, a back porch, and a side porch, a vegetable garden, a glimpse of the river, and tangles of wisteria and morning glories that might have swallowed the house whole if left to their own devices. My Rebel was already parked in the driveway next to the ancient Yamaha XS650 my new housemate, Matt, rode, and the CM250 I was towing was expected to take up residence against the weathered plywood fence for the time being. Matt was already outside when I pulled in. We didn't know each other well yet, but we had already bonded over our love of motorcycles, and there was something about him that felt familiar. In some ways he reminds me of my father: slight but muscular, bearded, with a goofy sense of humor, an uncanny knack for working with his hands, and an overwhelming reserve of kindness and generosity. The streak of rage that hides in my father is absent in Matt; he is prone instead to anxiety, quiet resentments, and self-doubt, vices we share and often commiserate over. Throughout the years that I've known Matt, he's become a precious friend to me—a resource of handiness, a compassionate confidant, and my favorite companion on an errand to the hardware store, a swim across the pond, a walk in the woods.

He helped me unload the motorcycle from the truck, and we rolled it over to the space we had cleared for it. The ultimate plan was to get it into the basement when it was time to winterize the other bikes, but when the frost finally started to bite that autumn, the gears had seized and we couldn't push it far. I fiddled with the gearbox a little but eventually gave up and left it where it was.

The other bikes, the Rebel and the Yamaha, we stowed in the basement without too much trouble. We packed away the gas tanks in big Tupperware containers to guard against spills and so that the smell of gas wouldn't stink up the house, then plugged the fuel lines with chopsticks and some Saran wrap. The house was built on a hill, and the basement was accessible from the downward-sloping side of the yard without the hassle of stairs. On the other side of the house, where the hill leveled out, was the driveway. To get the bikes into the basement it was a simple matter of a quick ride on the main road down to the neighbor's driveway, then up our narrow garden path and in through the defunct greenhouse door. The old CM, however, wasn't going to be moved easily with the gears locked, so it stayed where it was. I kept planning to mess with it some more, to figure out another way to get it inside, but eventually the snow came and enveloped it. It dropped to the bottom of my to-do list and, by the time I couldn't see it anymore beneath the drifts, off it completely.

THERE WAS ALREADY a jumbled workbench set up down in the basement, next to the washing machine and dryer, and we parked the other bikes within striking distance. I had planned to do some winter tinkering with the CM, but instead I spent a few lazy hours flipping through Clymer manuals, listening to the rattle of spare change in the dryer or the thud of the washing machine's spin cycle, admiring the slumbering motorcycles and dreaming of spring. Long fluorescent bulbs flickered over the bench, which Matt had dubbed "the office," where at least two ratchet sets, a dozen spray-paint cans, a busted violin, and jars of nails, screws, and drill bits crowded the surface. There was a grimy window to the right of the bench, looking out into the little greenhouse that was built onto the basement.

From my perch on a tall wooden stool I could see through this window and into the adjacent greenhouse, a view I became very accustomed to: the ripped plastic stretched over the windows, the stacks of empty plastic pots, the half-empty packets of seeds. There was a narrow path cleared between the basement door and the greenhouse door, but the rest of the greenhouse was filled with old bicycle frames, half-empty bags of fertilizer, what must have been fifty dollars' worth of redeemable bottles, and a vast collection of house paint, contents slopped all over the sides of the cans. Cobwebs hung from bulbless heat lamps and from between the seed trays. The black plastic roof seemed to be holding up against the elements, but that was about all the little greenhouse had going for it.

Despite its dilapidation, the space had captured my imagination when I moved in; the idea of a sunny, steamy room full of parsley and cilantro and flats of seedlings waiting to be planted thrilled me, but, as with the CM250, I never really managed to get things moving.

INERTIA IS DEFINED as *an object's resistance to change* in its state of motion. Newton's first law of motion states that an object must remain at constant velocity unless it is acted on by an external force. Like so many other terms in physics, inertia leads a double life. In its layman's form, inertia has a stagnant sort of connotation, one that implies laziness or slothlike behavior, a tendency to do nothing. When the term *inertia* is applied to people or organizations, it's hardly a compliment, and yet this connotation is far from the whole story; resistance to change is the most succinct way to quickly define inertia, but don't be fooled—an object doesn't have to be at rest for it to apply.

An object in motion is also affected by inertia, and it is this facet of the word that seems somewhat neglected in its standard usage. The motorcycle that rips past going over a hundred miles an hour has inertia the same way it would if it were parked in a driveway. Inertia simply describes the property of matter that resists changes in motion, whether it be at high speeds or at a standstill. It can be quantified by the mass of an object or by its momentum depending on the situation, but the principle itself is the same either way; if it's moving it will keep moving, if it's at rest it will stay at rest.

With the CM buried beneath a snowdrift and the Rebel hibernating in the basement, the stasis of winter reached out and snatched me, too. The ice on the river got thick, and the air became dry, almost brittle, like tissue paper against my skin. I spent most of my time indoors, studying and working, or in my car, commuting. I drove a boxy little Corolla that hurtled along back roads, mounted with tufts of snow and a surfboard rack, a relic of its California origins, the arcs of the windshield wipers and the dashboard heaters defined against the salted, ice-capped grime of the hood. I had never noticed the end of motorcycle season before, never thought twice about the sudden absence of deep, thumping rumbles on familiar winding roads, but that winter I missed them. I didn't miss them enough to find a way to include them in my life—like turning the heat down on a long-distance relationship instead of talking on the phone every day, I left my fascination for warmer months and an easier reunion. The scrape of the plow on the pavement outside my window didn't instill the same excitement that the roar of a two-wheeled, six-cylinder engine cruising by did, but I didn't dwell on comparisons like that for long; I had more than enough to think about. Icy mornings commuting to the university, the dark, muffled afternoons spent doing endless schoolwork, and those tiresome dinner shifts began to wear me down.

From my bedroom window I had a view of the road, and I would sit at the foot of my bed and consider the cars that stopped and started at the traffic light, frozen moments of conversation or contemplation spread across the tiny faces below me, shooting through the intersection and past the frame of my window. The movement within the cars below, relative to me at my window, all seemed slow and distant that winter. The weight of the snow seemed heavier than usual, and then in February Chuck died and it became heavier still. It's a perilous season, dark and cold, and sometimes it seems as though it will never end, as though it might actually swallow you whole. I think of Narnia, frozen in eternal winter by the White Witch, and the tiny talking animals that have given up on spring's sun ever warming their fur again. But it does. Winter will end. I repeated that to myself, over and over. It is the salve we New Englanders rub on our cracked hands and chapped lips when it snows in April or when it freezes in September. We must remind ourselves often: Winter will end.

I curled up at the end of my bed in a patch of afternoon light whenever I could, sometimes rushing home in anticipation of that precious last half hour of sun, before the cool blue light of early evening iced the trees and snatched that golden rectangle away, thrusting it behind the mountains. It softened the rawness of my arms and legs and face; it warmed my blood and nuzzled my eyelids, but it was never quite enough.

WHEN SPRING finally did come to Amherst the first year that I lived in the yellow house, I propped open the basement door and let the sun stream in through the ripped greenhouse plastic, illuminating a flock of tiny dust motes, like fireflies combusting in unison, lighting up the dim, chilled basement. The motorcycles parked just inside the door took on a soft glow. In the next few weeks the air began to warm, to melt around me like liquid glass. The ground softened. It gave. The roads turned to slop. The earth was being awakened like it always is, and this time I wanted to be awakened also. I felt the momentum of gathering heat, beneath my feet and in the air. I felt the leap and the lurch of the earth all around me as she raised her sleepy head. I wanted to wake up, too—*wake me up, too.*

Like a tangible answer from the earth, I began to develop a spring in my step, and it wasn't optimism; it was the sponge beneath my feet. Then there was a day that heated everything to the core. The snow shrank, the ice cracked, and I felt my heart rise at least a centimeter in my chest. I remembered, suddenly, that the trees would bud and then leaf, that the snow would melt, the grass would sprout. The days would be warm and pleasant and long. I thought of sun tea and ratty lawn chairs and cleaning out the greenhouse and taking my Rebel for the first ride of the season. I felt my toes begin to thaw for the first time in months. I willed the snow to melt, and I'm pretty sure it worked.

9.

Spacetime

I woke up the Rebel sometime in April. She sputtered at first, grunted sleepily, but soon enough she was alert, purring like a lazy cat. I let her hum for a few minutes to get the juices flowing while I ran inside and threw my Carhartts on over my shorts and dug my riding jacket out of a trunk in the attic. I wrapped the laces of my boots around my ankles twice, skipping the metal eye hooks in my hurry, and ran back out to the driveway. I slid my helmet on. My hair filled it like a soft cloud against my face, and I flipped up the visor to let in the sun. Traffic slid slowly by as I swung my leg over. A jogger ran past. I waited for an opening and then swooped out of the driveway, onto the road, like a bird of prey stretching her wings after a long sleep. The traffic light before the bridge turned green, and as I sailed through I looked over the railing and caught a glimpse of a fisherman leaning into the frothy current down below, mid-cast, with the water swarming around the tops of his waders.

It was the first hot day of the season, but on the Rebel everything felt cool. The wind slipped down my shirt and up my sleeves, and the chill was pleasant after spending the morning baking on the lawn, getting the Rebel out of the basement and ready to ride. I turned onto Bay Road and sped past a few broken-down barns and empty pastures, past a country ice-cream stand and a cornfield and a herd of cows stomping their feet on the other side of the electric fence. When I was a kid there was a big sloping hill just before my house where a herd of cows used to graze. "Hey, girls," my mother and I would say as we drove past them, because only girls get to be cows, and over the years it became kind of a ritual.

"Hey, girls," I shouted from inside my helmet, and then I let out a whoop because it was so beautiful outside and because you can do things like that on a motorcycle, by yourself, speeding down a country road, and not feel foolish. The season had begun, I had no place to be, and for a moment there were no cars in sight, no houses, nothing but space, and me, traveling through it. Space, the infinite area objects move in. Height, width, and depth: three dimensions within which matter exists. The cornfield on my left, the meadow on my right, the horizon ahead, the sky above, and the road behind me, reflected in my sideview mirrors.

I rode around Hadley farmland for an hour or two, got lost for a while, and eventually arrived home, almost by accident. After I pulled into my parking space and cut the engine, I climbed off and felt as though my blood was carbonated, bubbling up from the soles of my feet like soda pop, and it took me a second or two to find my balance. The hot metal tinkled as it cooled. Slipping the key into my pocket, I pulled a tarp over the Rebel and weighed the corners down with bricks. The bricks were warm in my hands from lying in the sun all day, and I just held them for a moment because the heat was so satisfying against my palms. There were barely discernible buds at the tips of the tree branches that swept out into the driveway, and I noticed for the first time that the backyard had developed a yellowy-green glow beneath the gray bristle left from the previous year. I love the way passage of time in New England is so beautifully evident in the land. A month doesn't go by without some sort of development in the scenery, leaves changing, snow accumulating, then melting, then becoming mud, then exploding with vegetation. I realized I hadn't noticed that particular yellowy-green growth before because it hadn't been there two days ago. Space without time is a stilled frame, and time without space is a stationary, sense-deprived eternity. Space and time are intrinsic to the way we experience reality, and they accompany each other without fail. It isn't such a leap, then, to consider them as part of a single continuum.

Spacetime is exactly what it sounds like—space and time considered alongside each other. In basic physics, this is unnecessary. Time is uniform, a universal constant. But when people began to think about the speed of light, and things moving relative to one another, revisions became necessary: space and time became flexible and inseparable quantities, because where velocities approach the speed of light, time's consistency falters. The spacetime continuum was born, a mathematical model in which the dimensions of space and time are both represented on the same plane. In spacetime, instead of mapping points in space, *events* are depicted. The additional dimension of time is represented, and so besides the where, you get the when. While the science is tricky, the idea itself isn't. Movement necessitates duration.

THE EFFECT of spring's arrival was intoxicating, filling everything with evidence of change. About the same time I got the Rebel out of the basement, I got a scholarship to study in Oxford, England, for the summer, and I could hardly wait to get on the plane. I had spent more time living in western Massachusetts than I'd spent in any one country since I was seventeen, and I was beginning to feel restless. The chance to go overseas for the summer was a relief, an expensive but crucial indulgence, so I started saving what money I could, signed up for courses in Shakespeare and writing, and soon after began to plow through the required reading lists. I kept time by the lilacs that grew close to the side porch, budding, coloring, then finally blasting open. I rode the Rebel until my inspection sticker expired in June, and then I rode a little more. I dreaded the thought of going back to Roy's mechanic shop almost as much as I hated the idea of getting a ticket, and staying off the bike was pretty much unthinkable. I guess I must have gotten a few illegal weeks into June before I finally rode out to Roy's. At least I knew where to park it this time.

I pulled up to the white line in Roy's shop, and he shuffled over to take a look, sullen as ever. He had reading glasses on the end of his nose, fastened around his neck with a piece of cord, and when he bent over to measure the tread on my tires I got the full view: the vertical dawn of his ass crack rising above the rippling horizon of his leather belt, oceans of denim beneath.

"Nope," he barked, after all of thirty seconds, and gave me a bemused, unimpressed sort of stare. "Better start walkin'."

I just looked at him blankly. "What?" I said.

"Start walkin'," he repeated cryptically, and I decided he must be joking. I smiled good-naturedly, and resigned myself to a little heckling about how worn my tires were. I already knew they might not pass, but I was expecting some leeway here. A "fail" sticker and ten days to fix it up, or something like that.

"No fail sticker?" I said.

"This is a motorcycle, honey. Different rules for motorcycles. The minute you fail inspections it becomes illegal to ride. Start walkin'."

The smile slipped off my face and down onto the greasy

floor. "Oh," I muttered, and started scheming. I was almost half an hour from home. No way could I afford to tow the damn thing, and, for that matter, no way was I sitting here all afternoon with this asshole, waiting for a tow truck. While I considered the matter, Roy went back over to his desk and started chatting with one of the salesgirls from the dealership showroom upstairs. The other mechanic had disappeared into the back room. I murmured something about getting it out of their way, then I turned the bike around and eased out of the garage, into the parking lot, and back onto the road. My cheeks were roasting red-hot inside my helmet, and I rode furtively back to Amherst, back roads the whole way.

I parked the Rebel in my driveway and left her there until I could find the money for the new tires, but there wasn't much time left before I was due in Oxford, and as I considered the conversion rate between the dollar and the pound, I began to suspect the tires would have to wait. Eventually, it was too late anyway; the lilacs had shriveled. I sublet my room for the summer months, packed a suitcase, and flew to London. The Rebel slept on.

ARRIVING IN THE UK that summer felt like revisiting the scene of a crime. I couldn't help but recall my seventeen-year-old self, running off to Ireland and living there for a year or so, drinking too much and doing too many drugs and smoking way too many Benson & Hedges cigarettes. It was a different country, a different accent, a different everything, but I hadn't been back to the UK since I was a teenager, and it put me in a nostalgic mood.

About forty years before, but in the same spot, my mother was also a young woman on her own, carrying a rucksack and traveling from place to place. It's strange the way knowledge of family histories sometimes remains dormant. When I was a child, the stories of my parents' lives were loosely known to me, but they seemed irrelevant. Then, when I grew older, they dawned on me all over again because I could see myself in them. My mother's summer spent wandering the UK on the back of a motorcycle was one of those stories.

In my first year living abroad as a teenager, the question I always heard was: What do your parents think of all this? The propensity for this particular question always mystified me. What does it matter, I would wonder to myself, what my parents think? They taught me to think for myself—to trust my instincts, to use my head, and to do what seemed best. Eyebrows were raised, worries were voiced, but there was never a question of receiving anyone's permission, and never the possibility that they would try to stop me. I wasn't eighteen yet, but they had never measured my capabilities or my independence with that yardstick. Both my parents have done their fair share of exploring—they didn't like that I was going, but they understood it.

When my twenty-one-year-old mother went on her own UK adventure, she left an apartment in Philadelphia and a job doing graphic design for an insurance company, all on a whim. An old boyfriend from high school was riding around Scotland on his BMW motorcycle, and he invited her to come and join him. She gave her notice and did it; they met in England. "First things first," he said, when he saw her. "Get rid of the suitcase." She put her things in his rucksack, and they rode to Stonehenge. The stones rose up in front of them, like cold celestial pillars, mysterious and familiar all at once. They spent a few weeks wandering together before the boyfriend had to go back to the States, taking his motorcycle with him, leaving the rucksack. My mother decided to stay and hitchhike, and so she went to Scotland and then Ireland.

She got plenty of rides, not to mention a few free dinners, and the hostels along the way were abuzz with drifting European youths. My mother has always made connections with new people so easily. She's personable and outgoing, and if she wants you to like her, it's practically a done deal. I've never managed new people with the same ease. As a little girl, I remember hiding behind her long skirts whenever I was being introduced to anyone, mushing my face into her thigh until I was sure no one was paying attention to me, then stealthily observing from behind the cracks between my fingers. As a young woman traveling, I kept to myself in the hostels, made polite conversation with people who gave me rides, but mostly I stayed in my own head, seeing everything, hearing everything, and storing it silently away until I could take it out and examine it when I was alone.

During my first week in Ireland I ended up in a small coastal town after a day of traveling with nowhere to stay. I had stopped there for a youth hostel, only to find it shuttered and dark, and as night fell I searched frantically for a place to sleep that I could afford. Finally, I found a room in a little bed-and-breakfast, more expensive than my budget allowed, but it was either that or curling up under my raincoat on the cold, wet cliffs, so I took it.

I gratefully followed the innkeeper into a room with a single bed, the mattress heaped with down comforters, and a mound of pillows spilling down from the headboard and onto the foot like a delicious goose-feather avalanche. She showed me how to use the hot water in the bathroom and left me in a cloud of steam. I melted into the shower and then into the mattress. The woman came in again after knocking lightly and gave me a plate of gingersnaps and a cup of milky black tea. I ate the gingersnaps and drank the tea, and my eyelids slipped down like shades being drawn by someone else. I slept and I had so many dreams, but when I woke up I couldn't remember any of them.

In the morning it took me a minute to recall where I was, looking at the pale, bright glow on the walls and curtains. Without my contact lenses everything was a blur, the folds of the draperies rippling into waves, the dark mound of my heaped clothes on a chair melting into a hazy mountain. I like this view of the world, where anything more than a foot in front of me is imperceptibly smudged into vague blocks of color and light, because it is totally private. No one else sees what I see in this myopic universe. Objects fade away and everything is finally, simply, just space and light. Looking up at the ceiling that morning, I reminded myself that I was beginning the most epic journey of my life to date. I breathed a sigh of excitement and terror and pride, then I swung my legs out of bed and got on with it.

WHILE MY JOURNEY BEGAN in Ireland, my mother's ended there. After the motorcycle boyfriend had gone and she was hitchhiking through small towns, there was one afternoon when she couldn't get a ride. She stood out in the rain all day, shifting her pack from shoulder to shoulder, waving her thumb at everyone who passed. Across the street she could see a little bed-and-breakfast, warm yellow lights glowing from every window. She stared at the front door for hours as the rain tunneled down the collar of her jacket, down her back, to moisten the waistband of her pants. Finally, as the dim gray afternoon began to grow even dimmer, she gave up on getting a ride, said damn the expense, and went into the B&B. She asked for a room, and was led to a glorious four-poster featherbed, made up with soft white linen and a stack of duvets. She peeled away her clothes and sank into the sheets and slept as though she would never wake. She did, though, twelve hours later, and suddenly knew that it was time for her to go home.

Before I began my summer studies in Oxford, I spent a few days in London visiting an old friend from Ireland, then I went to Cambridge for a bit. When I finally boarded a bus to Oxford, I had already begun to think of my own stories of Ireland, and also of my mother's, stories I hadn't thought of in years. I thought of her riding through the misty heath with her arms tucked around that faceless motorcycle boyfriend, and suddenly Stonehenge coming into view, and feeling the breath knocked out of her when she saw those towering stones. I went there and I looked at them, too, one weekend when a group of other American students were going. It was raining, but that seemed right somehow, to be wet and uncomfortable and shivering as I looked up at those rocks and wondered who put them there. Occupying that same space my mother had, it occurred to me that while there might be many miles between us, we were only one dimension away from each other.

That summer I spent a lot of time alone, happiest when left to my own devices. I walked around the city in circles, drinking to-go cups of hot tea and looking at architecture.

In my dorm room on the Trinity College campus I perched cross-legged on top of the desk to look out the window and into the gardens, where at night they would put on Shakespeare plays, though never the ones I was studying. I spent hours in the library, where there were long wooden tables with three partitions on each side and little desk lamps for each work space. There was a certain seat that I liked, where I left a pile of books and a note so that the librarian would know they weren't abandoned, and where a handsome Dutch grad student pored over mathematics texts across from me. Day after day, we would return to the same seats, whisper hello, and open our books.

There was an enormous window at the end of the table, so big there was a pulley system to open it, and in the afternoon the sun would slowly fall into alignment with the window until the book in my hands would burst into light, unreadable, each page glowing, and I would sit for a moment, enjoying that warmth with my eyes closed, then go to the window, draw the blind down, and continue with my work. I curled my bare feet around the wooden legs of the long table as I read, my toes twisting around the smooth grain like pink roots struggling for purchase.

At the end of the seminar I said good-bye to my classmates, turned in my keys, and went back to London. In London, I walked and I walked, and on the night before my flight home I went over to the house of my old friend from Ireland

and he made a pasta dish that glowed pleasantly in my stomach after I ate it, like swallowing a hot water bottle. Eventually, I made my way back to the other side of the city and into bed, where I took out my contact lenses, looked up at the dark, smudged ceiling, with the long, blurry shadows from headlights in the street, and knew it was time to go home.

10.

Power

When I returned from Oxford, I continued to struggle with the expense of new tires for the Rebel. My last year as an undergraduate had gotten its hooks into me by the time the leaves began to change, and finally the riding season had all but passed. As the snow fell, graduation came into view, and the relief to see it shimmering there, just a few months away, was palpable, but it was my mounting excitement for motorcycles, the drive to learn as much as I could about them and then get back on the road, that propelled me forward most of all.

By the time the snow had settled and the rumbles had disappeared from the icy roads, motorcycles were all I could think about. Being a student again had introduced me to so many things—Japanese, physics, books I'd never read, theories I'd never understood—but the most valuable thing I learned was how to work. How to set aside distractions and absorb knowledge; how to be unquenchably curious. This same kind of intrepid thirst had led me to Ireland, manifested as wanderlust, but as I threw myself into learning, both for school and for myself, I realized that I didn't need to wander to discover; I didn't need to be lost to find what I was looking for. The desire for geographic exploration was still with me, but it was tempered with the knowledge that I was learning to explore in different ways. I didn't have to leave the state or even the county to discover something new. Traveling overseas made me open my eyes a little wider, look a little closer, but I began to understand that it wasn't the distance or the novelty that made things feel so compelling, it was my own heightened capacity for observation—and that's a tool I can access anywhere, from my desk, from the seat of a motorcycle or while exploring a city I've never been to before, a country I've never visited.

My affair with motorcycles began as a fling, a way to rebound from Australia, but what I came to realize was that motorcycles were offering me more than just movement, a way from A to B. Like all great romances, these machines made me see myself and my surroundings with fresh eyes; they made me want to know more and to be better. Motorcycles were waking me up—just a nudge at first, hearing an alarm clock going off in the middle of a dream, then a full-body jolt, a bucket of ice water on my head. I realized that I had barely grazed the surface, that this flirtation could become my next great love if I let it.

I began to read everything about motorcycles that I could get my hands on. I read Clymer manuals and memoirs and histories of the industry; I read about engines and engineering, carburetors and countersteering; racing, cruising, dynamics, classical mechanics, I read it all. And the old motorcycle movies—I watched those, too, for good measure. *The Wild One*, *Easy Rider*, *On Any Sunday*, *La Motocyclette* with Marianne Faithfull and her skintight leather suit, with nothing, absolutely nothing, underneath.

Between the magazines, blogs, and online discussion forums, I was avidly tuned to anything to do with motorcycles. I bookmarked each Web page, bought every book, filed each fact away carefully until I thought that maybe I knew something—at which point, of course, I inevitably realized that I knew nothing, and I began again, from the beginning. It was a curriculum of my own making, a headlong rush to learn everything I could about motorcycles. It was work I didn't need to be doing, work outside the realm of assignment, of making a living, of meeting someone else's expectations. It was work born not of obligation but of fascination. The best kind.

MARCH ARRIVED; the snow shrank somewhat but still lay thick on my driveway, waist-high drifts on either side. My parents gifted me with a plane ticket to visit them in Florida for spring break, conveniently coinciding with Daytona's Bike Week, so I gratefully packed some artifacts of warmer days— my bathing suit, some shorts, a pair of flip-flops—and took time off from the restaurant. Before I left, I ordered new tires for the Rebel so that they would be waiting for me when I got back, then I headed for the tropics.

My flight to Daytona was full of bikers. The man I sat next to was from Pittsburgh, and he was having his motorcycle shipped down; he told me he made this trip every year, that the only vacations he ever took were to Bike Week. As he spoke, a stout woman with a shaved head, dressed all in leathers, walked down the aisle toward the bathroom. I grinned at my seatmate and started to feel good, like I was part of this strange club. Scoping the other passengers as they slept or knocked back Wild Turkey in plastic cups, I spotted no less than a dozen Harley sweatshirts, at least five leather jackets, a couple vests, and countless bandannas knotted around necks or across foreheads. I knew I was headed for a motorcyclist's paradise. I knew I was in good company.

Leaving the airport, I saw my father waiting for me in front of some palms. As I walked toward him, his eyes slid right past me. I gave him a wave and for a moment he looked surprised to see me, as if he was here waiting for his ten-year-old daughter instead of a twenty-three-year-old.

"Hey, Pop," I said, giving him a hug, and he murmured something into my shoulder about how grown-up I looked.

It's been said that I bear a strong resemblance to my father. We both have the same pink skin and blue eyes, the same thick, messy hair, the same round-cheeked smile. By then his hair was a little thinner, had gone a silvery gray, and his beard was snowy white. His glasses were smaller than they used to be, wire frames now, and his beard was cropped close against his neck. He wore his predictable uniform of khaki shorts and a pale blue button-down with a frayed collar and rolled-up sleeves, his socks pulled halfway up his spindly pink shins, shirt tucked in, a plain gray baseball cap tipped back on his head. He had a fresh, peeling sunburn across the bridge of his nose, and I could smell the ocean on him. He'd been out in his boat, he told me, fishing all morning. I asked if he had caught anything, but he hadn't. He didn't seem troubled by the fact. It was a beautiful day out on the water, he said, just beautiful.

On the ride home, three military jets shot by overhead in perfect formation, swooping and banking like a flock of sparrows. "They have a lot of air shows down here," my dad said, and told me about one he had gone to recently. He had been looking around in one of the merchandise tents when he found some hats he thought were pretty suave. They were black baseball caps with a little white Marines logo on the front, so he asked how much. The sales guy said they weren't for sale, and he pointed to a chin-up bar in the corner. Do ten of those, he said, and you get one free. I can imagine the skepticism with which the guy must have said this. My father is not a large man and not a young man; he's skinny as hell, not very tall, but he's worked hard his whole life and he's stronger than he looks. My dad cracked up. "You wanna see the hat?"

He didn't gravitate toward those Marines caps out of whimsy. My father served as a Marine during the Vietnam War, though he doesn't often mention it now. He has no veteran bumper stickers, he doesn't go to reunions, and he doesn't have any Marine buddies. When he returned from his tour of duty, people spat at him in the street in San Francisco, where he landed: a lone, scrawny military man, crew cut still freshly chopped, human residue of an unpopular war. He grew out his hair and his beard as fast as he could after his discharge. He started doing yoga. He learned to meditate.

It's about a half-hour drive to my parents' house from the airport. I had been there only once before. At first I was hesitant to visit them in their new home; I was still feeling sulky about the sale of their house in Vermont, I thought Florida was weird, I couldn't afford it, et cetera; but then I went, and of course loved it, have been visiting whenever I can since.

When we pulled into the driveway, I admired the periwinkle color they had painted the stucco, and the cobalt trim. I could see the fruit on my mother's citrus trees swelling in the front yard, blue glass bottles dangling from the branches of a live oak, and the bamboo she had planted along the back fence, which had erupted since I'd been here last. My dad couldn't wait to show me all the other improvements. He'd built an outdoor shower, a new fence, some shelves for his tools, a little patio. When he'd shown me all there was to see, we went for a ride on his motorcycle, a Suzuki V-Strom that he bought not long after I told him about my Rebel, and ended up at the beach. It was his idea to go and admire the ocean before my mom got home—admiring the outdoors has always been one of his favorite pastimes. We walked along the packed sand and dipped our feet in the surf, and even over the white noise of the waves I could hear the Harleys rumbling down Interstate 1. He told me he had been hearing the engines roaring late into the night, even though Bike Week had only just begun.

The dichotomy of my dad lies somewhere between the military and mysticism. On the one hand, he is harmless; a space cadet, as my mother says; a new-age goof. On the other, he is a Marine—nothing harmless about that. He's mellowed over the years, has buried that hard edge that I could always sense just beneath the skin when I was a child, but it's hard to forget. I remember a fierce argument my parents had when I was maybe six. I don't recall what the argument was about, and I doubt they do, either, but my father became so incensed he threw one of my mother's antique wooden chairs, hand-painted and inherited from her great-grandmother, down the stairs. It exploded on the landing below in a shower of wood splinters, and he stormed out of the house. The sound that it made as it shattered was like bones breaking. The next day my dad shut himself in his woodshop with all those jagged pieces and glued my mother's favorite chair back together. It took him all day, and when he was finished, it was stronger than it had been before, the hairline cracks barely visible, even if you were looking for them. This is how he was: first the rage, then the tender repair.

I used to imagine my father as a power switch: Dad On, Dad Off. In the On position, he was my favorite playmate; he would do anything to make me laugh, but then something would happen to flip the switch, and my father would disappear. Rage would bloom in his face, a deep, simmering, poinsettia red. The veins in his neck would bulge. His jaw muscles would dance in his cheeks as he ground his teeth together, his features distorted. He would become someone else, someone who looked like my father but was in fact a stranger. What frightened me more than this rage was the fact that I didn't know what would flip the switch, or how to flip it back.

This balance of power that I grew up with, the journey between the bookends of my father's repertoire, the destructive and the restorative, taught me to tread lightly. In physics, *power* is defined as the rate at which work occurs. It is a concept that hinges on the duration of work, and how much of it is accomplished in a finite set of time. On its own, work has no temporal implications. It takes however long it takes—but power hinges on time. The faster work is done, or energy transferred, the more power is being used. I think of emotions like rage and joy and despair, and the amount of energy these feelings exhaust, how abruptly they come, and how brightly they burn. I think of my father going from silly to wrathful in a matter of seconds, and the surprise of it, the utter shock. The faster the transition, the more powerful the reaction. As I grew older, the warning signs began to be more obvious, words became imbued with meaning, I started to see patterns. I quickly learned how to see the train coming, knew when to step out of the way, and his rage lost some of its power over me.

I don't like remembering my father in this light, because he's changed over the years, has fought to overcome the kind of trauma I can't even imagine. He's consciously and painstakingly evolved. He's a student of meditation, Pranic Healing, yoga asanas, good intentions; but the rage is hard to forget because it moves so quickly and is so all-encompassing, spreading across his face like wildfire. These days the On/Off switch is still there, but it's no longer the same seismic shift it used to be. I understand him better now and am grateful to have him, yet the scraps of my childhood fear will always cling to me: not fear of the dark or of serial killers, but of the people I love turning on me without warning and becoming unrecognizable.

My dad and I explored the fringes of Bike Week over the course of the next few days. Simply by nature of living in New Smyrna Beach we were in the thick of it, but we skipped the nightlife, which, by the sound of it, was raucous and inexhaustible. We did other things. We rode out to an event on the lawns of the Daytona Speedway; I was hoping for a race or a show, but it was mainly just a gathering of vendors and show-offs. The merchandise was nothing new, but the motorcycles I saw there took my breath away. There were the motorcycles being displayed, and those were cool, but then there were the thousands of bikes parked in rows ringing the event: bikes people had ridden there. I could've walked up and down those rows all day.

There were sidecars and three-wheelers and license plates from Maine and California and Texas; there were Harleys, so many Harleys, and seriously sleek sport bikes from Asia and Europe with lime-green racing stripes and exhaust pipes that were tricked out to spit flames. Vintage, brand-new, custom, stock, every make was represented, every model. I even saw a little Rebel 250, around the same year as mine, with Kentucky plates and 60,000 miles on the odometer.

When I couldn't look at the motorcycles any longer, I looked at the people. Bikers in chaps, in performance padded jackets, with Mohawks and ponytails and crew cuts and scalp tattoos; bull dykes with tits out to here; women dressed all in pink leather; a never-ending parade of middle-aged white men in black Harley T-shirts with varying degrees of hair loss. I saw a woman with no pants, just chaps and a G-string, then I saw another, without pants or chaps, just a hot-pink leotard and a pair of cowboy boots.

I spied my dad through the crowd as he looked intently at belt buckles. The lenses of his glasses had gone a shade or two darker in the bright sun, and he had his nose scrunched up as he peered into the display case. He had his button-down shirt tucked into his shorts. This is a constant, good-natured battle between us: I tell him to untuck his goddamn shirt; he tells me that he doesn't want to look sloppy. The tips of his ears were bright red, burnt to a crisp.

"Dad," I shouted, and I held up a T-shirt that said *69th Daytona Bike Week* and depicted a skeleton man smoking a cigar, holding a bottle of whiskey, and 69ing with a skeleton lady all at once. "I think you should get this." He laughed and shook his head, blushed a little. "Oh come on," I said, "it would look so good on you."

WHEN I WAS A LITTLE GIRL, I discovered my father's power tools. The bottom floor of the house I grew up in was his woodshop, but to me it was a different universe. It was a jungle of loud noises, of sawdust and steel, filled with smells of varnish and fresh wood and glue. I had a tiny wooden seat with four wheels that he made me, and I would race around the shop on it, paddling furiously with my stumpy legs, careening around the chimney, hiding behind the band saw. Sometimes my dad would push me around on it, and I would shriek with the excitement of it all. I loved to watch him work, the two of us wearing big padded ear protectors as he planed boards or power-sanded tabletops. Before long I noticed that the power buttons for most of his machines were round, green, and low to the ground—well within my reach. A new game was born, in which I would run around his shop and turn on all the machines. The noise was deafening, my father's dismay was clear, and I loved it.

The game was short-lived. To dissuade me, he would feign panic, then pick me up and run for cover every time I turned something on. His dramatic response, the sudden noise of the machine, the speed with which I was scooped up and relocated, stunned me. I didn't know what to make of it at first, but soon the game was no longer fun. His act frightened me, and it reminded me of his wrath although even then I could tell there was a difference. I stopped turning on the power tools. I continued to admire those big green and red buttons, one for On, one for Off, but I learned not to touch them. I imagined that everything must have this On/Off capacity. I puzzled over where this switch might be located on my father. Was it in his belly button? On his spine? Hidden between his toes?

My dad and I rode the V-Strom to Cassadaga a few days before I had to fly back to Massachusetts, a little town not too far from New Smyrna that is said to be the epicenter of some kind of psychic power—going there was his idea, of course. On the ride over, there were carcasses of burnt trees on either side of the road, like eerie hands clutching at the sky, the remnants of a brush fire that had swept through not so long ago. The smell of charred wood and wet, singed earth crept in through the vents of my helmet. Beneath the jagged black trees

MOTORCYCLES I'VE LOVED

new growth was emerging, rich, green shrubs that thrived in the ashes where their roots had found purchase.

When we arrived in Cassadaga we parked the bike in front of the post office and explored a little before finding a spot for lunch. Over crab cakes and coleslaw my dad talked about breathwork (one word) and the time he had spent at the Ananda Marga ashram in India after his discharge in the seventies. I sucked ice water through a straw and listened absently. My father has become practiced at verbalizing his emotions over the years, at releasing his feelings in a trickle rather than a flood—containing the power and processing it rather than letting it explode. He focuses his power on other things, on his passions. He becomes consumed with woodworking projects, with spiritual practices, books, camping gear, new tools, and, more recently, with his motorcycle.

I fished an ice cube out of my glass to crunch on and turned my attention back to my father, who was asking me if I remembered a rocking horse he had made me when I was a little girl.

"Of course I do," I said. I'm not sure how we got onto the subject of the rocking horse, but I am familiar with the leaps and bounds my father tends to make in his conversations. I follow as best I can. That rocking horse was beautiful, with a yarn mane and tail, painted by my mother like the night sky, a deep midnight blue, with silver and gold stars and the Milky Way across its wooden flank.

"You loved that," he said, and chewed for a moment. "And

135

do you remember the puzzles I used to make you on the jigsaw?"

"Of course I do."

My father's skills as a woodworker are vast. He can make practically anything out of wood: a jewelry box, a kitchen cabinet, a pergola, a letter opener—a house. As a child, I was unaware of this tactile genius. I didn't understand it. Beautiful, handmade things appeared throughout my childhood—a tree house, a rocking horse, a toboggan—but I never quite recognized them as my father's creations. My own strengths lie in my mind, and so this magic in his hands didn't register for me. I knew that he always smelled like sawdust, that practically all my toys came from his workshop downstairs, but I didn't know that everything he knew he had taught himself. I didn't realize that those shapeless lumps of wood I saw him carrying inside didn't just disappear—they became something else.

I may not have inherited his practical skill as a craftsman, but I gleaned something about the metaphysics of renovation from him: there's always time to rebuild, room to grow, and always, always more to learn. As time goes by, I realize that my father and I share more than I thought. There are minor differences: he builds with wood, I build with words; he pursues emotional knowledge and I go after ideas. But in the end we are both builders, and we are both in dogged pursuit of mastery. When I was younger I used to be frustrated when he would become so caught up in a new interest or hobby or project that he couldn't keep track of time. He would dive into the experience of learning, headfirst, without saving any room for logistics like making dinner or picking me up from soccer practice.

As I began to uncover my own capacity for learning, for losing myself in the exploration of something new, whether it be knowledge or terrain, I came to respect his; I came to admire his powers of fascination, of contemplation, and of illumination, and to strive for them in my own experiences.

11.

Energy

When I returned from Florida, the Rebel's new tires were waiting for me and the snowdrifts had shrunk while I'd been away. The fresh rubber smell of the tires filled the house as I ripped off the plastic and ran my hands over the tread. I called Matt, who had moved just up the road with his girlfriend, Katie, and who had promised to borrow a motorcycle lift on my behalf. He was my go-to motorcycle mentor at the time. The first words out of my mouth were "They're here!" and he knew exactly what I meant.

A few days later, we had the Rebel up on a lift, with a few mildewed paperback books we found lying around in the basement to fill the gaps between the frame and the lift. The spines of *Stranger in a Strange Land* and *The Sun Also Rises* stared back at me—such academic spacers, I thought to myself—while together Matt and I circled the heightened machine, mugs of tea in hand, tools at the ready, discussing our game plan. My faithful Clymer manual was on the floor next to my toolbox, which had grown in size and usefulness since my first foray into motorcycle maintenance, and Oscar Peterson's *Night Train* played quietly on an old CD player that buzzed a little in one of the speakers. I cracked open the toolbox, selected a likely sized ratchet, and set to loosening the rear brake caliper. Matt knelt on the other side of the motorcycle, and we took apart the puzzle, collecting spacers and nuts and bolts and screws and arranging them in what we hoped was a logical design on top of flattened grocery bags. When it came time to reassemble, this design would be the map. I wrapped my greasy fingers around my mug, drained the last mouthful of lukewarm tea, and set it aside. Matt slid the rear axle out while I held the tire in place, then we did the same with the front.

The process of mounting a tire on a wheel rim is a delicate one, beyond my skill set and accompanied by serious consequences if done incorrectly, so we nestled both the wheels and the new tires into the backseat of my car to outsource the rest to a mechanic. Once the tires and wheels were stowed, I removed the battery from its casing and hooked it up to a portable 12-volt charger. We called it a day and washed our hands with lemony dish soap and steel wool at the kitchen sink, then I put on a dress and went to work.

I let the battery charge overnight. It can be said that an

unused battery loses roughly one percent of its charge every day, so it's safe to assume a battery that hasn't been used for almost a year will need a little help. By running the engine, the battery is able to rejuvenate, to recharge itself, but without the mechanical energy of the pistons the electrical energy seeps away over time. When you come right down to it, the battery itself is only a means of storing energy, not generating it. The battery's charge is needed to start an engine, but once the engine is running, the battery is no longer actively being used—rather, it is being replenished. The charging system of a motorcycle varies with each model, but they all depend on a few components: the battery itself is one—this is where the stored electrical energy comes from when you turn the key. Second is the alternator—this is where the mechanical energy created by the engine is transformed into electrical energy. From the alternator, energy is sent out to the rest of the motorcycle but also delivered back into the battery. Third is the rectifier, which is responsible for regulating the raw electrical current that the alternator creates and smoothing out its distribution.

An engine needs a considerable jolt of electricity to turn over, but once it's running it no longer requires such a high voltage. Think of jump-starting a car with a dead battery—all you need is the initial connection to start the engine, the "jump," and then it's the engine itself that brings the dead battery back to life. The chemical energy of the fuel in concert with a spark creates the combustion within the chamber, which in turn creates the mechanical energy of the piston's movement, which travels to the alternator and becomes electrical. A jump-start is not unlike a kick-start, which is common on older motorcycles, but rather than using a rush of electrical energy to start the engine, the kick-start uses the jolt of mechanical energy created by the riders when they stomp down on the kick-start's lever. With a lawn mower, or maybe an old generator, there is a similar starting mechanism—the pull cord. Batteries, jump-starts, kick-starts, pull cords—they all serve the same function: waking the engine. The Rebel slept on in the shadows of the basement, but it was only a matter of time before she would be roused from her hibernation. Recharged, reshod, wide awake.

After the fresh tires had been mounted, Matt came over again and we put everything back together. We followed our imperfect map of operations, squinting at the manual as we tried to re-create the fuzzy black-and-white photographs. I slipped the battery back into its casing and refastened the power supply. When we were done we rolled the Rebel out of the basement, through the greenhouse, down the hill, and into the neighbor's driveway, where she sputtered to life without too much coaxing. After warming up the engine for a few minutes, I took her clumsily out into traffic, skidding on frosty gravel, taking the turn a little too wide, but feeling her lunge back into motion after a long stasis, awkward and glorious. Her tires touched road for the first time in their young lives, and the rest of her shook off the thick dust of the basement, all her parts moving together once again, a little loudly at first, a little stiffly, but before long it was as though she'd never been asleep.

Waking the Rebel did more than provide me with a different mode of transportation. It quickened the blood in my veins, the length in my stride; it signaled the arrival of a new season, a fresh start. Getting back on the motorcycle reminded me of how it felt to be fully charged and wholly invested—the sensation I had been pursuing with my research all winter was suddenly tangible. I could hear it, feel it, smell it. With my bachelor's degree in hand and two years of work, study, and little else behind me, I wanted a chance to take what I had learned out on the road and see how it handled. I had no idea what to expect from the unplanned years that stretched out in front of me, but I was ready to find out. Fully charged and with the Rebel purring beneath me, I started planning a new adventure.

12.

Impulse

That summer, I was approaching my twenty-fourth birthday, three years since I'd returned from Australia, roughly the same number of years I'd been gone. I was ready for a change. The idea of taking a long-distance motorcycle trip had been bouncing around in my head for months, and I was growing tired of Amherst, with its crushing, gray winters; I wanted new terrain. I was anxious to feel the uncertainty of travel, the thrill of arrival, the terror of saying good-bye.

As the summer wound down, I felt an urge, a physical pull that is all too familiar, and knew that I needed to leave. The rituals of comfort and stability began to seem binding, and the motorcycle in my driveway was the only thing that made me feel free. I'm not sure what attracted me more, the reality of being a motorcyclist on an epic journey or the symbolism of it, but in either case I latched on to the idea of riding south without understanding it or having any notion of what I was in for. Having never ridden farther than a hundred miles or so at a time, I had no idea what such a journey would be like, and I suspect it was the uncertainty that intrigued me most of all: the unknown narrative that awaited me.

As a seventeen-year-old I had traveled to escape, to lose myself, but as a twenty-four-year-old, I was traveling to find something. I didn't know what I was looking for, but that didn't matter—it was the search itself that I needed. My destination, I decided, would be my parents' house in Florida. Beyond this, I made no plan, had no ideas for what would come after. I would ride south, and that was all I knew for the moment; I focused on the journey itself. I began to search for a new motorcycle, one capable of going the distance and handling the interstate, and I started investigating places to stay, thinking about what route I planned to take. I rented a storage space for all the stuff I had managed to accumulate over the past few years, turned in my notice at work, dealt with the logistics of moving out of my house, and settled in to wait for the end of my lease.

They say the ability to control one's impulses is a psychological strength. A couple decades ago the Stanford Marshmallow Experiment gauged impulse control in a group of four-year-olds by giving them each one marshmallow, then promising them two if they could wait twenty minutes to eat it. Checking back years later, researchers discovered that the four-year-olds who were able to delay the gratification of eating their marshmallow grew into more dependable and better-adjusted adults—they even scored higher on the SATs. I wonder how my four-year-old self might have reacted to this experiment. I mentioned reading about the study to my mother, and she told me that my brother, Phineas, would have popped that marshmallow into his mouth before they'd even finished explaining the directions.

"You, on the other hand," she said, "would have spent those twenty minutes weighing your options." It's possible she's right, but I think she might have reversed the order of my thought process. Having a deeply analytical reaction to the world around me hasn't made me a patient adult, nor has it quenched my impulses. Personally, I think I would have eaten the marshmallow, and *then* spent the next twenty minutes analyzing my decision. Regretting it, justifying it, savoring it. For the most part, I follow my impulses without questioning them—it's only after the fact that the left side of my brain raises its hand and begins to systematically rip apart the choices I couldn't help but make.

THE SEARCH FOR a new motorcycle took a little time, but eventually I found an ad for a 1982 Honda Silverwing GL500, with no picture and just one line of information—the year, model, mileage, price—and below it, the words *call Gerald* and a number. I reached for my phone. The man who answered was monosyllabic, and he responded to my questions with deep, rumbling yeses and nos.

"Could I come tomorrow?" I asked.

"Yes," he said.

"Could I come around two o'clock?"

"No," he said.

"Three?"

He paused. "Yes."

"Great," I said. "I'll see you then."

"Yes."

I dragged along my friend Seth for company. When we arrived at the address in Worthington and got out of Seth's car, Gerald appeared, looking precisely how I had pictured him. Somewhat grizzled, with a scratchy white beard and tufts of silvery hair going in every direction, he hobbled down to his driveway to where we were already inspecting the Silverwing. It was a beast of a motorcycle, well over five hundred pounds, almost thirty years old, with a cigarette lighter and radio speakers contained within a hefty fairing that was so big it looked more like the dashboard of a Buick than a motorcycle's instrument panel. The body was a rich, chocolaty-red color, with two hard plastic saddlebags to match, each of them printed with the word *Interstate* and studded with square red reflectors. I swung my leg over and centered the weight of the bike. I was on my tiptoes, not the best sign, but I wasn't about to give up that easily.

"Mind if I take it for a spin?" I asked.

"Go for it," Gerald said.

Riding the Silverwing was about as different from riding the Rebel as it gets. It was quiet behind the big windshield, and while the engine didn't have much punch to it, there was no question of its highway ability—it was, after all, the Interstate model. I made a sweeping U-turn and headed back the way I had come, playing with the gears, slowing down, then speeding up to get a feel for things. By the time I pulled back into the driveway, I knew I wanted it. I also knew it was too big for me. What the hell, I thought, and bought it anyway.

As Gerald filled out the title and wrote me up a bill of sale, I could barely sit still. I arranged to come back for the bike itself the next day, but we exchanged the paperwork and the money and the keys right then and there, then shook hands to seal the deal. The Silverwing was officially mine.

The next day, it poured. I waited for the sky to clear, but it never did, so it wasn't until the day after that I got a lift back to Worthington. I had the Rebel's license plate with me, and when I went to fasten it to the Silverwing I was pleased to see that Gerald had left me the nuts and bolts to do this, a detail I hadn't thought of, and the nuts were shaped like little silver skulls with molten red plastic eyes. It seemed like a good omen at the time, like those two little skulls would watch over me—a pair of hoodlum guardian angels. I waved my ride off and started the Silverwing. I got on and remembered how very high the seat was. I suddenly began to worry that this might not have been the best idea, but it was too late for that, so I stubbornly blocked it out. And it was such a handsome machine. I pulled out onto the road and once I was moving I pushed my worries away and got acquainted.

Learning to ride the Silverwing was like learning to ride a motorcycle all over again. The sheer size of it—the weight, the height—all conspired against me. In the first few days of owning it I dropped it twice just trying to park the damn thing. I found that only under the best circumstances could I find enough purchase with my toes to back it up, and that I couldn't manage to pick it up by myself—in addition to weighing well over five hundred pounds, it was unwieldy and top-heavy. Both were troubling realizations in light of my plans for the coming months, but I stuffed my doubts down as deep as they would go and told myself that it was just a matter of time and practice before I would be able to handle the Silverwing with as much ease as I could the Rebel. Besides, every motorcyclist has heard the saying "It's not *if* you drop it, it's *when*." I hung on to that, and kept riding.

AUGUST SLIPPED AWAY and I turned twenty-four. I started by packing my books first, then I packed my trunk with most of my clothes and took down the artwork I had hung. With empty bookshelves, an empty closet, bare walls, and two weeks left on my lease, I continued to wrap up the loose ends of my life in Massachusetts. The uncertainty of when I would be back to claim everything spurred me on, and the more excited I got, the higher the tower of cardboard boxes climbed.

I took the Silverwing to a mechanic to get it checked out. I had found a different shop since my last run-in with Roy, one with a showroom full of bikes made all over the world and a staff that was kind and professional and helpful. I gave the guy behind the service desk my keys and asked him to give the Silverwing a once-over. The price I paid Gerald for it fell short of my budget, so I had figured on spending the difference to get it up to speed—after all, a thirty-year-old motorcycle can use all the love it can get.

"I'm riding to Florida," I said, "and I sure would like to get there. Also, if you could lower the seat at all . . . even an inch, that would be great."

"No problem," the guy told me. "I'll call you in a few days."

With the Silverwing in the shop, I slapped its license plate back onto the Rebel and rode that around in the meantime. At first I couldn't believe it was the same bike—it felt more like a scooter after my time on the Silverwing, but it was a relief to feel my feet flat on the ground once more, even if it did seem like a downgrade.

I think it must have been one of my last days at work when I got an update on the Silverwing. I remember sitting out in front of the restaurant with Zach, the head chef, before dinner service started. He was smoking and I was sunning, with my legs stretched out into the street, trying to soak up those last few minutes of freedom before the dining population descended. My phone buzzed inside my apron and I answered it.

"We've got a 1982 Silverwing here," the man on the other end said.

"Yep, that's mine," I told him. "What's the verdict?"

"Well," he said. "We looked things over, and—it's pretty old. I'd figure it's a good bike for cruising around town, but that's about it. I can't really say if you'd make it to Florida on this thing, but I guess I advise against trying. Just enjoy it for what it is, y'know? There's not much we can do for it. Anyway, you can come pick it up whenever you like."

"Hm," I said.

"Oh, and the seat's as low as it can be."

I said thanks and hung up. Zach lit another cigarette and held it between his teeth while he rolled up the white sleeves of his T-shirt over faded tattoos that snaked around his biceps. We sat for a minute, watching the pedestrians stroll by.

"What's the story?" he asked me.

"Weeell," I said. "He would advise against taking it on such a long trip."

"But you knew that already."

I glowered at him, but that was true. I did know that already. How could I not know that? A thirty-year-old motorcycle is not exactly the ideal cross-country vehicle, even if it is the Interstate model. A beautiful woman walked past and our heads turned simultaneously to watch her go. Zach pushed his sunglasses up onto his nose and grinned at me, his snaggle-toothed smile cracking open his tired face.

"And?" Zach prompted me. "You're gonna do it anyway?"

"Yeah," I said. "I'm gonna do it anyway. I'll get as far as I get, and if it breaks down, then I'll cross that bridge when I come to it."

"Sounds like it's settled, then." He finished his second cigarette and put the filter in his pocket. "Tell you what—if you break down north of the Mason-Dixon, I'll come pick you up and bring you back."

"What a relief," I joked, although the prospect was more terrifying to me than funny, and we both got up to go inside. Again, I pushed my anxieties away and gave Zach a thump on the back as the door slammed shut and the air-conditioning hit us. "Ready?" I said, meaning the dinner shift, but still thinking about my ride south. Then I scooped up my helmet from where I had left it on the bar and tucked it away in the basement.

THERE IS ANOTHER FORM of impulse this makes me think of, and it has nothing to do with the sudden and unreflec-tive nature of my decisions. The physical manifestation of im-pulse has to do with the length of time a force is applied, and there is no better example to illustrate it than the design of a motorcycle helmet. The goal of the helmet is to increase the amount of time during which one's skull absorbs impact, thereby reducing its impulse. A force that is applied over a short period of time would be far more devastating to the brain than the same force if the impact were prolonged by mere fractions of a second. The padding of the helmet, combined with a layer of Styrofoam underneath, both prolongs the impact and disperses it, thereby lessening the likelihood of traumatic brain injury. Should a person's head connect with concrete instead of the inside of a helmet, the chances of a head injury skyrocket. In the event of a crash, motorcyclists are almost fifty percent more likely to die if they aren't wearing a helmet. Impulse is the reason why.

It's also worth mentioning that motorcycle helmets are designed to absorb impact only once—this is because the layer of Styrofoam, which is crushed during impact in order to prolong and disperse the force applied to one's head, doesn't rejuvenate, it can't un-crush itself—and so the next time that helmet is in a crash it won't slow the impulse the way it is meant to. Impact will be almost as severe as if the helmet wasn't there.

Consider the math. An impulse of one hundred newtons per second is enough to cause a fatal brain injury, and an average head might be expected to weigh six kilograms. Based on these numbers, a motorcyclist not wearing a helmet would need to be going only 37 mph at the time of a collision for a fatal head injury to occur. Now consider: you are thirty-seven times more likely to die in a motorcycle accident than in a car accident.

Thirty-seven miles per hour. Thirty-seven times more likely.

THE NEXT DAY I got a ride to the mechanic's shop and picked the Silverwing up, then rode to work. I was in the middle of setting the dining room when the sous chef called me over to the big windows in the kitchen that looked out over the parking lot. He pointed down at two police officers circling the motorcycle, parked side by side with the dumpster. "I think you're getting a ticket," he said with a bemused grin, but I was already racing down the steps, into the basement, and through the dish room. The two officers looked at me quizzically as I crashed through the screen door and into the alley.

"Is there a problem with the bike?" I asked them, breathless. "Because I can move it." They looked at each other and then back at me.

"*You* ride this?" one of them asked in disbelief. I nodded.

"Should I move it? Is it okay to park it here?"

They started to laugh in unison. I waited.

"So should I move it or not?"

"No, no. It's fine," the other one said. "We were just looking."

I breathed a sigh of relief and went back inside. Through

the screen door I heard them say, "Would you believe that?" as they strolled away, their thumbs hooked on their utility belts, caps tipped back on their heads. "She's *tiny*."

I went back upstairs and couldn't decide whether to smile or swear. Was I flattered or insulted? And, more to the point, was I brave, or just an idiot for thinking I could take this enormous, ancient motorcycle all the way to Florida and expect to arrive intact and unharmed? Here lies the crux of motorcycles. The point where reason ends and courage begins. Get it right and it's the purest, most exhilarating balance that ever was. Get it wrong and the consequences are dire— no need to ask why motorcyclists are called organ donors, why mothers warn their children to stay away. It's what the motorcycle-safety class instructor Joe meant when he called me both brainy and ballsy, and it's what Rigdhen meant when he told me if I wasn't at least a little scared of motorcycles I was crazy, or a fool, or both.

I had started out thinking that I would accomplish the journey I had in mind through sheer willpower, but lately I couldn't help but wonder if maybe reason had fallen short, and this was an impulse I shouldn't have followed.

13.

Vibration

I had some doubts about riding the Silverwing south, but I was committed to the trip by then and didn't seriously consider backing out. As I got more comfortable handling the new motorcycle, the dread ebbed and a sense of exuberance swelled. The internal alarm bells never stopped clanging, but they softened, became background noise, eclipsed by excitement. I began to pack for my trip, setting aside the essentials that I would take with me as I boxed up the rest. I unhooked the hard plastic saddlebags from the Silverwing, brought them upstairs, and packed them like twin suitcases to make sure everything would fit, then left them in the corner of my room as the rest of my belongings dwindled.

I was familiar with the process of paring away everything but the necessities, and in fact that summer it was easier than it had been in the past. In this instance, my things would be waiting for me when I came back to retrieve them, whenever that was, but in Galway, Ireland, five years earlier, I had gotten rid of everything permanently—everything except the contents of my backpack and my boyfriend—then flown to India.

As I prepared to leave Massachusetts years later, whenever anxiety reached out and grabbed me I reminded myself of that particular journey. The globe-trotting antics of my teenage self impressed me by then, but in a detached way, like looking at someone else's photo album. If she could do it, I thought, flipping through mental snapshots of Kolkata and Sikkim and Delhi, then I can do it, too. Memories of India didn't set me at ease, because it hadn't been easy, but they gave me a sense of faith in my decision. They reminded me that it wouldn't be perfect, but at least I had learned a few things since then. India was hard and it was worth it—I felt lost while I was there, scared, but also alive, and then afterward, I felt more awake for having gone. I think of India as an incredible book that I read when I was too young: even though I didn't fully understand it, I learned what I needed to know at the time. And, if I'm being honest, I should really read it again. Something that I have discovered about leaping into the proverbial deep end is that although I might not have any idea where I will land, or how, I always land somewhere.

The last few days of August arrived and the final stages of

moving out had to be tackled, not the least of which was the fact that I had not one, not two, but three motorcycles in my driveway. The Rebel, the CM, and the Silverwing, all in a row. The CM was worth next to nothing at that point, and finding an amateur mechanic to come haul it away was a piece of cake. I rejoiced to see it go—by then it was only a reminder of my failure to do anything but dissect it, and while it had helped me understand the innards of a motorcycle somewhat, my grand plans to make it run had fallen flat on their unrealistic faces. The Rebel, on the other hand, felt like an old friend, and I wanted to make sure she found a good home. The head chef, Zach, had been admiring her for months, so when it came time to find a buyer, he was my first choice. We haggled a little—he tried to soften my asking price with promises of restaurant gift certificates. "Zach," I scoffed at him, "you already feed me for free." We finally agreed, and we made plans for the switch-off.

I rode it out to his place in Chesterfield. This was disguised as a favor, but really I just wanted one last day of riding the 250. "Home delivery," I said, when I pulled up. "How do you like that?" He gave me his snaggletoothed smile and showed me the spot in his garage to park it. I even passed along my Clymer manual, though part of me wanted to keep it, having spent so much time poring over it, but I was feeling generous that day. I handed over the keys, signed off on the title, and that was that. "I'll take good care of it," he promised. I gave the Rebel one last affectionate slap on the gas tank, then we hopped into Zach's car and he took me back into town.

The last gasp of moving out was suddenly upon me. The house had to be cleaned, the remnants of past tenants dealt with. There was a yard sale that spanned an entire weekend and swallowed the front lawn, and the final harvest of the garden, which yielded more kale than I knew what to do with. Matt loaned me his truck, and with it I drove all my worldly possessions to the storage space I had rented. It was the smallest, cheapest unit I could find, and it was only with some help and a little ingenuity that everything finally fit inside. After cramming the last truckload in, I pulled down the door, clicked the padlock shut, and took a breath. I was officially a nomad, and there was only the Silverwing to concern myself with now.

WHEN I HAD FASTENED the saddlebags back onto the motorcycle and strapped down the rest of my gear, it was time to go. I went over a mental checklist to be sure, searching for anything I might have forgotten, anything I might be missing, but there was nothing. I was ready. I started the Silverwing, got on, and with a touch of the throttle and a gentle easing out of the clutch, my toes left the ground and I was off.

As I coasted down the lumpy driveway, I quickly realized that something felt very, very wrong. The handlebars were jerking back and forth, practically leaping out of my hands. I blamed the ruts in the road and kept going, putting all my muscle into keeping the front tire straight, and I succeeded, but just barely. As I gathered speed, the frantic wobble began to smooth itself out. Then by the time I hit pavement it was only a mild vibration, and the faster I went, the smoother it became. I breathed a sigh of relief. That was weird, I thought. For the next few miles I took the machine through its paces, searching for some clue to the vibration, but found nothing.

It was only when I approached a four-way stop and had dropped to under 15 mph that I felt it again. There was a car in front of me, a car behind, and two others waiting for their turn at the stop sign. I wrestled with the handlebars, giving it everything I had to keep the wheel straight, but the slower I went, the more violent the shaking became, until I was almost at a complete stop and suddenly the Silverwing flew out of my hands, dumped me unceremoniously on the asphalt, and fell on top of me.

A fallen motorcycle is a terrible thing to behold. So terrible, in fact, that just thinking about it makes me feel ill. I have seen a few motorcycles this way, and it never gets easier. It always hurts to look at it, but in the moment—if you're the one who's dropped it—there is adrenaline flooding your body, blurring your thoughts. What especially hurts is to remember it after the fact, when everything is in slow motion and there is no biological distraction. I close my eyes, and suddenly there it is—a machine known for its speed, its agility, its raw power, only on its side it has become just another hunk of metal. Like a crippled horse or a capsized boat: the worst has happened and shame rushes in. In the moment, the task of getting a fallen motorcycle upright dominates, but in hindsight, the fall happens over and over, like a scratched record stuck on a hideous note.

Motorcycles have fallen on top of me before. In fact, this particular motorcycle had fallen on me before. But in traffic? That was new. As I squirmed out from underneath it, people appeared on all sides, asking me if I was all right, if I was sure, if I was *positive*. I slipped my helmet off and assured them that I was fine, willing myself to vanish into the craggy pavement as two men heaved the bike back up and rolled it onto the grass by the side of the road. I shook off the shock of losing control as best I could, and stammered something about the vibration, about the handlebars leaping out of my hands, trying to make sense out loud of what had happened; trying to recover some small semblance of dignity when the road refused to open up and swallow me. A particularly distressed woman continued to ask me if I was all right every twenty seconds. The two men who had lifted the bike left me in the hands of this very maternal woman and drove away. Eventually, I convinced her that I really was fine, that I didn't need any more help, and thanked her profusely for her concern until she, too, got into her car and drove away. The four-way stop was suddenly empty. I took a breath and sat down next to the bike. The implications of what had just happened came over me all at once, and it was only until I managed to shove them all away that I could see my immediate problem. What now?

I called Matt, and to my tremendous relief he answered. I explained what I could, and suddenly with his familiar, concerned voice on the other end of the line, my throat tightened. "Where are you?" I asked him, in what I hoped was a casual tone. "On my way," he replied without hesitation, and hung up. I've never been so relieved, nor have I ever been quite so grateful. I found some shade underneath a tree and waited. Another motorcyclist came through the intersection, saw the bike parked on the grass, and stopped. "You okay?" he shouted. I gave him the thumbs-up. "Everything's fine," I shouted back, and forced a smile. He gave me a salute and roared off. I said it again, quietly, just for me: *Everything is fine.*

Vibration isn't generally desired. In almost any kind of machine, vibration is a sign of something gone wrong, a clue to imbalance, or unwanted friction. In a few instances, such as music, vibration is favorably cultivated, but in so many others it's the reason for an appointment at the repair shop or the prelude to a blowout. The unfavorable vibration is a mysterious and worrisome pest, hiding inside the coffeemaker, the muffler, or at the bottom of a glass of water as a *Tyrannosaurus rex* approaches. More technically speaking, vibration is an oscillation around an equilibrium, an interruption in the balance. There's a lot to be said for balance; I clearly still have some things to learn about it.

FIVE YEARS EARLIER, after teaching English in India but before moving to Australia, I spent a little time in Thailand. Thom was with me for most of that period, but he went on to Melbourne a few days before I did, and I had some time to myself. My last night happened to be New Year's Eve, and as I sat alone in my hotel room, my suitcase open on the bed while the last few hours of 2006 slipped away, bombs began to go off all over Bangkok. The city itself seemed to vibrate from the intermittent blasts. I could hear them in the distance, but for a time I didn't understand what was happening— didn't know what it was I was listening to. In America, my mother had caught wind of the Bangkok bombing head- lines almost immediately and was frantically searching for more information, unable to reach me. In Thailand, I knew even less than she did. I sat cross-legged on my bed, watching the news in another language, trying to understand exactly what was going on. Feeling the building shudder, wondering if fireworks could be that loud, or that close. As I watched the picture on the television fuzz up and then sharpen, fuzz up and then sharpen again, I tried to understand what was hap- pening. I tried to understand how it was that I had gotten there in the first place, on that day of all days, and where it was that I was going. I wondered what had gone wrong, what had tipped this delicate balance, and what it would take to set it right again.

FIVE YEARS AND half a world away, I sat cross-legged under a thick maple tree, looking at the Silverwing and waiting for Matt, struggling to understand the same things.

14.

Aether

By the time Matt's truck pulled up beside me I had stomped down hard on my ballooning hysteria and put my game face back on. The immediate problem, of what to do with the Silverwing, was all I had the energy for. There was no way in hell I was getting back on that machine just yet—I was shaken, and I was afraid that if the vibration happened again I wouldn't be able to stay in control of the bike. I was too freaked out, and all I could think about were the numerous stop signs and traffic lights between where we were and Matt's house—it seemed clear to me that dropping under 15 mph was what had caused the Silverwing to buck me, and I knew that was unavoidable.

Matt listened to my feeble diagnostics and offered a few ideas of his own. The luggage packed too high seemed like a possibility, or a cupped front tire, or a loose ball bearing, but none of it really altered the fact that things sometimes go wrong on motorcycles, especially old ones, and I was riding a motorcycle that I couldn't physically wrestle through a problem like that. Matt volunteered to ride the bike himself while I drove his truck. It was only several miles to his house, he reasoned, and he had a couple inches on me, a few more years of riding experience, and more muscle to back it all up. We transferred my gear into the truck, and then Matt started the engine and took off. I followed him, my teeth clenched, knuckles white on the steering wheel, watching as the handlebars jerked back and forth, then became still as he gathered speed.

He made it without any catastrophes, to my great relief, and parked the bike at his house in the center of Amherst. I pulled up next to him in the truck. "Success!" I cried, and he hopped off the bike. We discussed the problem some more and I did a little of my own research, but the more I learned, the more I realized that the problem could be almost anything. As I read stories of "high-speed wobble" crashes—*wobble* being the technical term, and low-speed and high-speed being the two choices—I came to understand that I was actually pretty lucky getting the low-speed variety, otherwise I would have almost certainly been testing the limits of my barebones catastrophic health insurance plan.

As it happened, Matt and his girlfriend, Katie, were heading out of town that very evening and would be gone all weekend. They offered me their room while they were away, and I gratefully accepted it, having no place else to go. After they left, I took a shower and inspected the many scorches and bruises, new and old, that dotted my legs and hips, then fell into bed and unleashed the emotions I had subdued over the course of the day. I stewed in my own anxiety for an hour or two, then slowly, fitfully, drifted off to sleep.

OVER THE COURSE of the weekend I got in touch with my friend Rigdhen and asked him to give the Silverwing a once-over. He swung by and took a look at the machine—I told him what had happened, but he had no immediate ideas as to what the problem might be. He shrugged and said, "Maybe it was a fluke."

"But," he added, "that motorcycle is no good for you anyway—there's another motorcycle, out in Holyoke, that you should see." Rigdhen knew the guy who was selling it, and said we could go check it out the next day. I conceded. The possibility that the Silverwing wasn't the right bike for me was something I had been pushing away for weeks, but recent events made this sinking suspicion impossible to ignore.

I've never been good at admitting defeat, and although the realization that I would be a fool to press on with a motorcycle that I could manage only under the best of circumstances was hard to accept, accept it I did. There would be questionable roads, heavy traffic, crazy drivers, and plenty of getting lost—there would be situations I had yet to even imagine.

The unknown was no place to be going on a motorcycle I didn't trust and couldn't control. The moment I decided to sell the Silverwing, the relief was palpable. The knots in my stomach loosened, the tightness in my jaw went slack. I decided that I was not admitting defeat, that I was simply using my brain. It had taken an accident on the very day of my departure to wake up this common sense of mine, but once I dumped the Silverwing in the middle of the road there was no turning it off. Willpower was not going to make me any taller, and willpower was not going to make the Silverwing any more manageable. It was over. I never rode the Silverwing again.

FOR CENTURIES there was a theory pursued by the scientific community called luminiferous aether: the medium of light, said to be a substance scattered throughout all of space. It was said to be fluid, without mass, incompressible, and transparent. As experiments were done, contradictions arose, and the theory became more and more complex to accommodate them: for example, aether had to be rigid enough to propagate light but also elastic enough to not have any effect on the movement of the planets. The harder aether became to prove, the more fantastic the theory had to become in order to explain it. The experiments done up until the beginning of the twentieth century all failed to provide proof of aether, at that point a theory deeply ingrained in the consciousness of modern science, yet the assumption of its existence persisted. It wasn't until Albert Einstein reasoned that perhaps the so-called failed experiments were in fact successful that any headway was made. If aether didn't exist, then the complications that had arisen by trying to force a false theory to match up with the laws of physics fell away.

In 1905 Einstein proposed the theory of special relativity, which argued that the speed of light is the same no matter what time or place it is observed from, that there is no mythical substance that transmits light, merely a simple set of laws that govern it. This is in fact what the "failed" aether experiments had been pointing to all along, but it took abandoning an attractive theory in order to see it clearly. The Silverwing had seemed so perfect in so many ways, like an indestructible highway chariot, but ultimately the hypothesis was wrong— the numbers didn't line up, and I began to search for another machine.

IT BECAME CLEAR that it would take me longer than a weekend to sort out my mode of transport, so before Matt and Katie returned from their weekend away, I moved my gear to their attic, where an old mattress and a rickety bed frame were hidden beneath layers of trash and junk and things in storage. I threw some stuff away, stacked some other stuff in tidy towers, aired out the mildew, and before I knew it the room looked livable—cozy, even. There was an empty door frame leading to nowhere that was covered with a torn screen, and more than one window was missing its glass, but as long as the warm weather held, I had a good place to hide out while I searched.

The motorcycle Rigdhen took me to see had been sitting in a basement for years, glimmering in its gloomy corner like an open flame. It didn't run at the time, but other than that it was in pristine condition, a 1995 Honda Magna, candy-apple red. It had barely 6,000 miles on the odometer, 750cc's of displacement, and a seat height that fit me perfectly, leaving both feet firmly on the ground. Before the title and the money changed hands, Rigdhen and I hauled the Magna to Northampton to get it back into working condition—in other words, he worked diligently, cleaning carbs, replacing the air filter and the spark plugs, while I pestered him with questions and ran errands at AutoZone. After two days of working and waiting for parts, we started it, and I heard it run for the first time. It was a beautiful, dangerous sound, like a lion's roar, or the snarl of a brush fire.

I went back to Holyoke, got the title, and paid the guy, and after that the Magna was officially mine. I transferred the license plate from the Silverwing and made sure to switch over those little skull-shaped nuts as well. Their plastic red eyes were the same color as the Magna's paint job; it seemed lucky. When I rode it to Amherst I could hardly believe how quickly it responded to my touch, how seamlessly it moved across the road. There was so much power available, I was going 50 mph before I had to change from second gear to third. As Rigdhen would say: it had serious balls.

I took the Magna back to Matt's house and parked it next to the Silverwing. Side by side, the Silverwing towered over the Magna—it looked twice the size of it, and yet where the Silverwing topped out at 80 mph or so, I have never found the Magna's limit. The next day I called a tow truck and took that sweet old highway sow over to Rigdhen's garage in Northampton, where he had agreed to sell it on my behalf. Suddenly, the disaster began looking more and more serendipitous. I had a motorcycle that suited me, and that would get me to Florida without dying of old age. I had been so attached to the Silverwing, in all its retro glory, that I hadn't noticed it didn't fit the equation.

The only problem now was that I no longer had any saddlebags, and with the smaller motorcycle came less room for luggage. I went back to my storage unit and dug out a blue duffel bag, then quickly realized that I was going to have to get rid of some gear. I went back to the storage unit again and dropped off everything that didn't make the cut. The remaining items I managed to stuff into the duffel bag and my backpack, then with my tent, sleeping bag, sleeping pad, and rain gear I crafted a handy little backrest. When I was finished cramming everything onto the bike, I had a sizable mound where the passenger's seat used to be and a snug little place just big enough for me to slide between the gas tank and my gear. I had already gone to the RMV and transferred the Silverwing's registration over to the Magna. My insurance was updated, my paperwork complete. For the second time that week, I was ready to go.

15.

Singularity

Although I was ultimately journeying south, I began by heading north for a few weeks to clear my head. My destination was northern Vermont, on the outskirts of a little town too quaint for its own good. On top of a mountain and a few miles west of the village green, there's an old cabin that's been collectively owned by my mother's side of the family for more than a century. It is affectionately known as "the bungalow," perched at the top of a treacherous dirt road, afflicted with deep potholes, washed-out ruts, and the occasional fallen tree branch. It's incredibly isolated up there, without electricity, phone lines, or neighbors. The way up the mountain becomes impassable when the snows come, and even during the warmer months it is a steep and troublesome stretch of road. Spending time up there alone is a singular experience—

solitary, and also extraordinary, like nowhere you've ever been before.

After less than an hour on Interstate 91, I was over the border and into Vermont. The Magna was handling beautifully, though without a windshield, traveling at highway speeds was brutal. I thought of the Silverwing wistfully, with its enormous windscreen and bulky fairing, its bottomless gas tank, but the moment I pulled off the highway for lunch and set both feet flat on the ground to park, I knew I had made the right choice. I resolved to order a windshield and pick it up on my way back through western Massachusetts, then bent my head into the wind, crouched down low, and made the best of it.

As I went north I saw the catastrophic effects of Hurricane Irene, which had overwhelmed the entire state of Vermont near the end of August. Covered bridges were washed away, chunks were taken out of the roads, and houses on the brink of collapse teetered all along the riverbanks. I rode past a little diner that was a childhood landmark, where I had been eating clam chowder and slurping chocolate milk shakes since forever, only to find it gone—a pile of soggy rubble in its place. As I continued on toward the bungalow, I began to have doubts about the road leading up the mountain, started wondering what I would do if I couldn't make it. It would be a long walk for help if anything went wrong. I pressed on; it was the only thing to do. Eventually, I reached the beginning of that last mountainous stretch of road and turned off the bike. The trees rustled their leaves at me, and I saw a deer bound away through the underbrush. The sudden quiet after the incessant rumble of the motorcycle was soothing against my eardrums. I unlocked and opened the gate, then walked up a little ways, trying to gauge the difficulty. The road seemed miraculously unharmed. In its usual state of disrepair, but no worse than I had come to expect. I went back down to where the Magna waited and restarted the engine, then began my ascent.

I went as slowly as I dared—while speeding up the mountain wasn't the plan, neither was taking it too slowly. With a motorcycle, the accelerator is a friend on steep, treacherous ground: lose momentum and you're toast. I gritted my teeth and gave it my best, roots and rocks throwing my front wheel all over the place as I zigzagged around the largest obstacles. What I can only assume would have been a thrill on a dirt bike was genuinely terrifying on a heavy street motorcycle, loaded with a bunch of extra weight, but when the trees opened up to reveal the plateau on which the bungalow was built, I felt a rush of exhilaration. My shoulders were in knots from gripping the handlebars so fiercely, my hands ached, and my lower back had been screaming since White River Junction, but none of that mattered. I had made it, and I could see for miles.

As a child, I would go there, mostly with my mother, though sometimes my dad and my brother would come, too, and we would all stock up on library books and groceries and art projects before ascending the mountain for a week during the summer, maybe two. We always seemed to be there for my birthday in August—I remember a cake shaped like a bunny head with string licorice for whiskers, and one with icing the color of twilight: soft pink and dusky blue swirls. My mother went there as a child—my grandfather, too. At this point the land is collectively owned and managed by more than a dozen cousins and second cousins and cousins once removed, but when the bungalow was built, in the early 1900s, it was my great-grandfather who commissioned the construction, Henry S. Brooks—Brooksie, they called him.

There are old photos and portraits lining the walls of the living room at the bungalow, a spread of Brooksie's descendants. My grandfather as a boy, sketched in pencil and colored charcoal, next to sketches of his three siblings, and my mother and her sister, rendered in two oil paintings; their five cousins on the opposite wall. The dust lies thickly on the picture frames and the air in this room is stale, like the contents of a time capsule. The idiosyncrasies of four generations crowd the bungalow's walls, cupboards, and drawers. Yellowing notes written in bossy tones, old maintenance logs, chipped china and musty doilies, mutilated board games and endless redundancies in three drawers of rusty tools, a few raggedy fur coats in one closet, an old cot in the other. The singularity of the bungalow lies not only in its isolation but in the peculiar personality that emanates from its beams, the composite of at least a dozen relatives who have etched themselves into this building in one way or another over the past century.

The sun was beginning to set as I unpacked the Magna. I heaved my duffel bag onto the west-facing porch then sat next to it, watching as the mountains in the distance turned indigo and the sky became a dusty pink, the smoky blue clouds cracking open like an egg to reveal the yolk of the sun, molten orange, dripping down behind the horizon. I admired the silhouette of my motorcycle set against the panorama of mountains in every direction, and then I brought my things inside before the light disappeared altogether.

I set my gear down in one of the two bedrooms, then began to light the kerosene lamps. I left one next to my bed, another in the kitchen, and another near the fireplace, where I busied myself lighting a fire to soak up the chill in my fingers and in my toes. The crumpled newspaper smoldered at first, then burst into light, illuminating the room and flickering across the old family portraits that lined the walls and the farming artifacts that perched along the ceiling beams. I went into the kitchen and heated a can of soup on the gas stove. The sound of my spoon against the bottom of the pot made a quiet, metallic rasp, and I kept stirring it just to hear that soft scraping—so peaceful.

In the living room the fire popped suddenly, then settled back into a static whisper, the wood shifting occasionally. With the relative quiet of the mountain, the tiniest sounds stepped forward, and a whole new layer of white noise became apparent: the crickets; the wind; the house itself. My own small sounds seemed to become smaller still when I heard the echo of a large truck downshifting on Route 101, miles away. But this particular kind of smallness—this cosmic insignificance—I have always found comforting. In this sense we are all small, we are all alone, and I felt content to hear the shallow thumps of my own movements, set against the deep buzz of the outdoors, and the urgent, transcontinental breath of the wind.

IN PHYSICS, a *singularity* is an exception to the rule: a point in the spacetime continuum that defies the laws of physics as we know them. One of the basic tenets of physics is that its laws are constant and universal, but a singularity is a point in space where these laws can't be applied. Black holes emanate from singularities, concentrated centers of infinite mass. Considering the contradictions of infinite mass is only the beginning— by association, other infinites come into play, including infinite force, infinite momentum, all sorts of things beyond the scope of what we can understand. A singularity is like a bookmark—a placeholder for something we can't yet comprehend but that we know exists. Essentially, all we know is that we don't know much.

They say the universe itself emanated from a singularity: the Big Bang. A moment in spacetime when a point of infinite density exploded outward, becoming the universe as we know it. A concentrated moment of both endless existence and utter destruction, all bundled together in one cozy little speck of matter. There's something about being at the bungalow that makes me more inclined to think these big, universe-sized thoughts. Most things seem inconsequential when you're up on the mountain. I think it must be the uninterrupted view of the sky that does it, how at night you can actually see the creamy swirls of the Milky Way, and sometimes, if you're really lucky, the shimmering, opalescent curtain of the aurora borealis.

I poured the soup into a cracked porcelain bowl and took it into the living room, where I ate it, watching the flames rise and fall, listening while the wind howled around the mouth of the chimney and chased puffs of smoke into the living room. I read in the dim light for a few hours, then dragged the screen in front of the fireplace and started getting ready for bed. I brushed my teeth with bottled water, wrapped myself in musty wool blankets and my sleeping bag, and blew out the kerosene lamps. The fire still crackled softly in the living room, and a cricket couldn't have been far as I drifted off to sleep.

WHEN I WOKE UP the sun was streaming in through the windows, and past the open bedroom door I could see the kitchen, which faces east, glowing with brand-new yellow light. I heaved a deeply satisfied sigh, rolled over, and didn't wake again until almost noon. The bungalow inspires sleep, reading, and little else—a welcome break from the rest of the world. There is nothing up there but history, trees, birds, and, of course, the sky. Eventually, I shuffled out onto the porch with a cup of tea in my hands, and I sat. My thoughts wandered, I finished my tea, and still I sat, watching the clouds melt. There was a monarch that stayed close to me, sailing this way, then that, always with the wind. I felt at home.

My parents lived in Vermont for thirty years, but in a sense I am the only true Vermonter among our little clan, born and bred. My brother was born in Montana, my mother in New Jersey, my father in Michigan, which just leaves me. Now that the rest of them have relocated, Vermont doesn't feel like home in quite the same way it used to—there's no house to draw me back, no family to return to—but there is something about just being there that feels familiar, and there is always the bungalow, where some of my oldest memories took place. Something about Vermont's quiet towns, her rotting, red barns, the way old men in pickup trucks lift a hand from the steering wheel to each car they pass on a lonely road, speaks to me of home. I get this feeling, like my roots are buried somewhere deep beneath my feet, but that they aren't connected to anything aboveground anymore. They don't grow; they're just there, marking the place where I sprouted. I feel their presence and I feel their severance in equal measure.

The sun was on my face, and the wind nipped at my bare

toes. The nostalgia faded, and thoughts of the journey ahead began to emerge. I strung up the hammock and lay there for a few hours with a book of crossword puzzles, then I went inside and made a pot of rice, heated up a can of kidney beans, and wished for an egg to fry or a handful of spinach to wilt. Alas, groceries hadn't been part of my luggage plans. I pawed through the cupboards, finding some mismatched nonperishables—instant coffee, powdered iced tea, pancake mix, canned green beans, popcorn kernels, bow-tie pasta— remembering that at some point I would need to go down the mountain and bring back some real food, and that meant braving the treacherous road all over again. I stalled for a day or two, but eventually I had eaten what was edible and down I went.

To my great relief, going down was less difficult than that first time going up. I had already made a point of remembering the most difficult patches of road, and one particular pothole that would have been an instantaneous game-over had my front tire fallen in, so I knew roughly what to look for and where. I made it down without too much trouble, visited the overpriced local grocery store, and checked my e-mail at the public library. Stocked with a backpack full of provisions, I headed back up the mountain, again without too much trouble. It was when I was already at the top, turning the motorcycle around on the slippery wet grass, thinking I was in the clear, that I went down. The engine stalled and I lost my footing simultaneously, and for the second time in a week I had a really heavy, really hot piece of machinery fall on top of me. The smell of my blue jeans melting against the tailpipe was all I could think about as I got out from underneath it, hit the kill switch, and sat down next to my heavy fallen steed, knowing full well that there was no one in my proximity to help. I let loose an inconsolable wail, and the echo must have traveled for miles—the romance of singularity clashing with the reality of being alone on a mountain.

After a few futile efforts to lift the motorcycle up off the ground, I sat down and caught my breath. There is a certain method for lifting heavy motorcycles, which goes like this: you squat with your lower back against the seat, feet shoulder-width apart, one hand on the handlebar, swung in close to the body, other hand gripping somewhere stable near the back of the bike. Then, the idea is to press your butt against the edge of the seat and lift with the legs, pushing back with the butt, and walk it up bit by bit. The motorcycle needs to be in first gear so it doesn't slide. They say even a grandmother can lift a heavy bike like this, but I couldn't manage to get it off the ground. Maybe it was the wet grass, the incline, or the fact that my feet kept slipping out from underneath me right when I had the full weight of the bike in the air—or maybe that line about the grandmother is a load of bullshit. Either way, it didn't work, but I wasn't ready to give up. There had to be another way.

I had an idea. I went over to the porch, found a thick block of firewood, and brought it over. I lifted the motorcycle as high as I could with the method described above, kicked the wood underneath the bike to prop it up while I readjusted my feet, then lifted it a few more inches, pushed the block farther back toward the tires, and from there I walked it upright, flipped out the kickstand, and there it sat, good as new. I flopped down on the grass next to it, pulsing with adrenaline and feeling joyous, but also tired, right down to the bone, and emptied my lungs in what might only be described as a victorious battle cry. For someone who is often accused of being quiet, creating a sound so ragged and raw felt strange, and somehow important, as though I had just uttered bold truths in another tongue—as if I'd just had a fight with Goliath and won. It didn't even matter that there was no one around to tell.

There is an incredible amount of satisfaction in sharing that vista with no one, and I felt a fresh surge of it as I sat next to my raised motorcycle and surveyed the mountains. I love cooking for one on the gas stove, and bathing on the east porch beneath the solar camping shower, strung up with a pulley, not a soul for miles to see me dancing and shivering as I rinse my hair with rainwater. I love reading on one porch, then standing up, turning sloppy cartwheels on the lawn, and moving to another porch to keep reading. On clear, warm days I would go stomping around the meadow, following forgotten, intermittent paths, absently picking bouquets of

Queen Anne's lace and goldenrod, then throwing them back into the field. When it rained, I built enormous fires inside, so that if one were to look out the window the misty drizzle and the wood smoke would twine together and it would be impossible to tell which was which. My motorcycle, slick with mountain rain, would blaze through the fog like the beacon of a lighthouse, its red gas tank shining through the thick white air. On days like that it was as though I were caught in a cloud—come to think of it, I was.

I stayed on the mountain for almost two weeks. I thought of the generations who had stayed there before me, my grandfather in particular, and I thought of a story he had told me once. When he was a younger man there had been dirt bikes kept up there, the same sort of 60cc or 90cc bikes he eventually bought for his daughters. There was a web of logging trails throughout the woods surrounding the bungalow, but with a good pair of tires and a little luck, a trail wasn't even necessary. On one ride, however, luck hadn't been on Gordy's side, and he'd strayed from the trails. Somewhere out in the woods he hit a fallen tree, hidden by the undergrowth, and went flying over the handlebars. The bike had refused to start after he brushed himself off, and so he trooped back to the bungalow, looking for a little help towing it home. When he returned to the scene of the accident with a few other guys, they couldn't find the dirt bike anywhere—they searched for hours, but it was gone. Eventually, they had to give up, scratching their heads. It was almost as though the universe had folded in on itself for a moment, creating a split-second singularity, an inexplicable event within spacetime, which happened to suck the matter of one small motorcycle through a wormhole and into another, incomprehensible dimension. Either that or the damn thing's still out there, covered in moss, forgotten among the rocks, and the trees, and the dirt.

16.

Propulsion

From the bungalow, I crossed into New Hampshire and stayed with my mother's sister and her husband, my aunt annie and uncle Woody, for a few days. The return to civilization was as satisfying as the departure had been. I traded solitude and mountains for endless, scalding-hot showers, television, and the Internet. I slept in a soft bed and ate food cooked by someone else. I watched movies. I checked my e-mail. It was glorious. Before long, though, I was ready to go. I still needed to swing back through Northampton to pick up the windshield I had ordered, and I could feel the season beginning to turn. Halfway through September, the nights were getting cold and the foliage was coming out: time to head south.

I talked to my dad while I stayed in New Hampshire, and he eagerly offered to meet me in Virginia on his own motorcycle so that we could do some riding together. At first I didn't want to. I felt protective of my adventure south. I wanted to do it alone, without help, without company. When I went abroad at seventeen I had no friends to visit, no contacts, nothing but the maps and my own whims to guide me, and this had seemed like the right way to go about it, like the experience was worth more because it was so lonely. As I considered the journey south, I began to wonder if I might not enjoy having my father along for part of it—if there might not be a different sort of value in inviting him to join me. I wasn't looking to lose myself anymore, I was setting out to find something, and it occurred to me that sharing this adventure with my father could be part of the treasure hunt. So I invited him, and he got serious about packing. So serious, in fact, that my mom called me the day before I left New Hampshire to tell me about it.

"Lily," she said, "there is a tent pitched in my living room." She sent me a picture to go along with this claim, and I saw that it was true. My father had spread out his entire arsenal of camping and traveling items in a grid on the floor, and there in the middle of it all, a medium-sized tent was pitched, complete with rain guard and ground cloth. I was still laughing when he got on the line and started telling me about his GPS system, and how he had rigged it to fit on his bike, and how he wasn't going to take his camping stove, because we probably wouldn't use it much, et cetera, et cetera. It struck me that I was going to be traveling with *the* most prepared man on the planet. It was a comforting thought—but I wasn't there yet. It was a long way to Virginia.

I made my way back down to Massachusetts slowly, trying to diminish the beating I was taking from the wind. I stayed in Florence for a night, then the next day I rode over to my friend Seth's house in Northampton and set up a little living room nest for myself there. He said he could use the company, not to mention the fact that he had a Honda Super Sport 750 parked in his driveway—it drew me like a moth to the flame.

The next day, I picked up my windshield. When I ripped open the box, however, I realized that while the windshield itself was all I had hoped it would be, the mounting brackets were not included. I called around to the local parts dealers to see if they had what I needed in stock, and no one did. Defeated, I ordered the mounting kit, which was of course very expensive, and settled in to wait for a few more days, until the part arrived. During this time Seth showed me some of his favorite back roads, and we spent a few autumn afternoons flitting through the hill towns of western Massachusetts like fat red hummingbirds. The leaves had begun to turn in earnest there, and the trees were exploding with color. One afternoon we stopped at a little roadside eatery called the Snack Shack and ate shrimp po'boys while we admired our motorcycles, one new, one old, both red.

After a few days, I got the call that the brackets had arrived and I went over to pick them up. I fastened the mounting brackets, slotted in the windshield, and loaded up the motorcycle. I had been taking everything on and off so frequently that by then I was becoming increasingly familiar with where to put it all and how to strap it down. I was done in no time. I used a wrinkled roll of blue painter's tape to stick my directions to the gas tank, where I could look down and reference them when I needed to, then Seth and I rode over to my favorite coffee shop. We sat outside and I admired the Magna, piled high, while we drank our coffee. The sun was in our faces, and the fallen leaves were swirling around our feet. I drained my cup and stood up to go. I wasn't quite sure where I was going to spend the night, but I knew it was time to get started.

"I'll see you when I see you," I said, and got moving.

It started out as a beautiful day. I took a road I'd never ridden on before, and headed west toward the Taconic State Parkway along Route 66. The trees stretched out overhead like a smoldering, leafy awning. It was the end of September by then, and the colors were vivid. Burnt sienna and carmine red, gold and umber, and the thick needles of the evergreens bristling in the background, sliding into one long smudge of color as I whipped past.

Propulsion is the means of creating forward motion. In Latin, *pro* means forward and *pellere* means to go, or to drive. As I forged ahead on my journey south, leaving the stillness of the bungalow behind and opening up my engine, letting it propel me across Massachusetts and into New York, I thought of other cross-country journeys. My own, as a twenty-one-year-old returning to a home country that didn't quite feel like home anymore, and my brother's, propelled west with such venom, such confusion that I don't think even he understood why he was moving or where he was hoping to arrive. And yet, for all the reasons I have to be angry with my brother, many of them fell by the wayside when I wasn't looking. In the years since I'd seen him on the West Coast, he'd become a small but persistent part of my life. We didn't talk often, maybe once or twice a year, but they were awkwardly pleasant conversations and he sounded mostly even-keeled and healthy. The proselytizing gave way to biblical scholarship for the most part, and my disinterest in discussing religion and conspiracies no longer needed to be reiterated, it went without saying. We learned to talk about other things, and although that repertoire isn't large, we're working on it. It still feels like speaking with a stranger, but a friendly stranger; it's encouraging.

I didn't notice at first, I was moving too fast myself, but I eventually saw that Phineas had stopped his wild propulsion away from our roots some time ago, and was in fact drifting back in the direction he'd come from. He's a different man of course, but that's okay—I'm different, too. Perhaps it was my own propulsion that kept us so far apart for so long, but now, rather than drifting apart, we are moving incrementally closer.

When we were young my mother made us matching capes that fastened at our throats with Velcro and were emblazoned with our initials on the back. I picture those two mismatched kids, the gangly, black-haired boy next to his girl-shaped, goldfinch-sized sidekick, and I think of them blasting off in different directions, capes flapping in the wind, stubborn fists stretched out overhead to punch through the air resistance, and I realize afresh that we're not all that different.

WHEN I HIT the New York border, the sky opened up and fell on me. The rain was torrential, soaking me from above, and then jumping up from the road and soaking me from below, too. I was drenched in a matter of seconds—there was no time to pull over and don my rain gear, and once the rain had begun there was no point. I was already as wet as I could possibly be. What I didn't realize was how cold I was about to get. The farther I went, the more violently I shivered. Since I had chosen a secondary road to take me through New York, widely skirting the city, the places to stop were few and far between. At first I kept going because it felt safer than pulling over. The pounding rainfall was making road shoulders and turns hard to see in advance, and if I kept going I could ride in the riverbed left by the tires of the car up ahead, hopping on the coattails of their momentum. Later, when the rain slowed and then stopped, and the road was slick but no longer flooded, it seemed like I might as well forge ahead. It wasn't until the sky darkened and my hands became numb within my waterlogged gloves that I began to look for motels.

I pulled into the first place I spotted, but found it utterly deserted. The sign remained, but the motel was long gone, an empty row of boarded windows and padlocked doors. I turned around in a driveway thick with mud and went back to the road, disheartened. I kept going, beginning to wonder if I would ever find a place, until eventually the word MOTEL emerged from behind some trees. I stomped down on my rear brake and swung into the parking lot. The sign said STAR BRITE MOTEL and the neon was lit. I heaved a sigh of relief, parked the bike, and rang the bell next to the door labeled OFFICE. I waited for almost ten minutes, and rang the bell twice more before a little old woman pushed aside the lace curtains, peered out at me, then opened it.

"Oh," she said, "you're so wet." She had a thick German accent and a little apron on over her dress. "Come in, come in—you'd like a room, yes?" I nodded weakly and she guided me inside. I handed her my credit card without even asking how much. As she led me back outside and down the long row of rooms, she eyed my motorcycle and asked me about my trip. "Oh! All by yourself?" she exclaimed. "How brave, my dear, how brave. Me, I've never been on a motorbike, not once." I told her maybe she should try it, and she responded, "Oh, no, I'm much too old for that sort of thing. But you— you're young. Motorbikes are for young people." She offered to let me park the bike underneath the overhang, just outside my room, but by then I couldn't care less if it got wet. I thanked her anyway. She told me there was a diner just down the road a piece, and so after I unloaded the Magna and took a shower, I walked there. I'd had enough of the motorcycle for one day.

The Rainbow Diner was every bit what I was expecting: red vinyl booths, a pie case, and grizzled old men at the counter. I ordered the roast beef dinner, which was enormous, swimming in gravy, and came with a bowl of cream of chicken and rice soup so thick my spoon stood up in it. I ate what I could, which was roughly half of everything on my plate, and hurried back to the motel so that I could crawl between my scratchy starched sheets and close my eyes.

The next day I got up, chose the least wet pair of jeans available to me, and set to repacking the motorcycle. The old German woman waved as I strapped down my last bungee cord and came over to say good-bye.

"You are to have a safe trip," she commanded. I nodded.

"I will certainly do my best."

She squeezed my arm and went back to cleaning rooms. My gloves were still soaking wet, so I tucked them under one of the straps to dry in the wind, then turned the bike around and headed back to the Rainbow Diner for breakfast. The waitress, a different one this time, told me there was a waffle and egg and bacon special for five dollars, so I said, sure, lemme have that, then got out my map and traced my way down into Pennsylvania. A silver-haired man and his grandson two booths away were checking out my motorcycle, and after a minute he called over to me, "Hey—that thing yours?"

"Yup," I said.

"Where ya goin'?" he asked. I told him Florida, and he let out a little whistle from behind his teeth. My breakfast arrived, and again it was so huge I could barely finish half of it. He asked me if I needed any help with directions heading out of town; I said no, thank you, I think I've got it, but he scribbled down a couple things on a piece of yellow paper anyway. As I was finishing my watery coffee he started telling me about a tree-house hostel in Georgia that one of his sons had gone to. I told him it sounded pretty cool, because I am a sucker for tree houses, and he said that if I felt like giving him my e-mail address he'd make sure and pass along the website for it.

I paused, but he was a sweet old guy having breakfast with his grandson, and I liked the sound of the hostel, so I wrote it down for him. After I finished my breakfast and paid the check, I gave him and his grandson a smile and headed out. When I started the bike I could see them both waving furiously at me through the window. I revved the motorcycle extraloud for the kid, who went nuts, then I raised a hand at them and pulled out of the parking lot.

ALTHOUGH THE MORNING was clear, there were still deep puddles on the road from the heavy rain the day before, some more like rivers than puddles, so by mid-morning my feet were soaked again—not to give the impression my boots had actually dried overnight, because they hadn't.

I had crossed over into Pennsylvania by the time the torrential rain began again, appearing out of a clear blue sky like a magic trick, and this time I was on a two-lane highway headed toward Philadelphia. When my tires started hydroplaning across the road I slowed down, crouched behind my windshield, and struggled against the suction of enormous trucks whipping past me, waves of water crashing into my left side. I struggled to find the safety of someone else's wake, but the road was too busy, with too many lanes. It would have been best to pull over, but there was nowhere obvious, and moving at a diagonal through the quickly moving water was treacherous, so I kept going. The rush of traffic and the water beneath my tires had sucked me up into its chaotic flow. As the highway became a river, all of its travelers seemed to become one. An enormous, snaking body with more momentum than any one vehicle could possess alone.

Forging ahead, I endured the battle into the late afternoon, when the rain eased and the sun emerged, somewhat sheepishly. I took my next exit, which spit me out near a shopping plaza, and swooped around the parking lot until I spotted a Starbucks. It would have to do, I thought to myself, and parked.

When I peeled myself away from my motorcycle, it felt something like removing a Band-Aid very, very slowly. My back was a twanging mess from the way I had been crouching behind my windshield, and my fingers were white raisins. The day had miraculously turned sunny and warm, so I unstacked my tower of luggage to try to find something dry to change into. I quickly realized that nothing I owned was dry, and so I picked a few of the least damp things out. As I walked across the lot to the Starbucks, my feet squelched inside my boots and I looked back to see watery footprints following me across the pavement. I went inside and into the bathroom, leaving a slug trail of mud and rainwater in my path. Stripping off my jeans, I wrung them out in the sink and crammed myself into my other, slightly less wet pair. I slipped the thermal lining into my leather jacket and squirmed out of my T-shirt, replacing it with a scratchy wool sweater. My socks were disgusting. I threw those away, and held my feet underneath the hand dryer for a few minutes, one by one in an awkward stork pose, then slipped on my other pair of shoes, which were rubber-soled and made mostly of cloth. These were not ideal for a motorcycle, but then—nothing about my situation was ideal at that moment.

I emerged from the bathroom with a wad of wet clothes in my hand and got a cup of coffee, then I sat at the counter and went over my map. The guy next to me was giving me some curious glances out of the corner of his eye, so I leaned over and asked him if he had any sage advice for getting into whatever suburb I was aiming for. He gave me some directions—then the guy two seats down looked over and gave me some different directions. I feigned gratitude to them both, went outside, and called the friend I was going to visit. He gave me some altogether different directions, which I scribbled down and taped to my gas tank.

Two hours, a few wrong turns, but no major disasters, later, I pulled into my friend's driveway somewhere in the Philly suburbs and received a warm welcome, a hot shower, good company, and dinner. I spent a lovely weekend in Pennsylvania, and when Monday rolled around I was excited to be back on the road and headed south again. There was no rain when I left, but it was so cold I had to stop every twenty miles and run hot water over my hands in public restrooms to regain feeling in my fingers. Through Maryland and West Virginia the windchill was brutal, but by the time I finally crossed over into Virginia I was too numb to notice, going too fast to care.

I found my exit and turned off into the rural pastures of Virginia. From there it was just a few more miles to my second-cousin Vail's house, where my father was waiting for me, and even though my fingers were frozen, I was dying to pee, and I hadn't stretched my legs since Maryland, I kept the throttle open. I almost missed the turnoff, but saw the street sign at the last minute and slammed on my brakes, skidding onto a long gravel road that went on and on, until finally I caught a glimpse of my father's motorcycle at the end of it and knew that I had made it.

17.

Reaction

As I got off the motorcycle, I saw my father and Vail walking in the pasture near her horse barn. The pasture was vivid green, and a mist rolled in toward the house in slow white plumes. The smell of sweet, wet grass rushed at me as soon as I took off my helmet. They strolled over and my dad wrapped me up in a big hug. I've never been so relieved to see him. After a moment, my dad released me and patted me on the head, as one pats a beloved dog. He's always done this. As a teenager, I managed to somehow be offended by it—as an adult, it felt like an unbearably sweet gesture made by a man who has never fully been satisfied with the effectiveness of his own words.

I gave Vail a hug also, and she practically lifted me into the air. Vail is at least ten years older than my father, and probably half a foot taller. She's a buxom woman, with an iron-gray bowl cut and a broad smile, always wearing black Velcro shoes and jeans pulled up to here. She lives alone in a big, cluttered house in rural Virginia, and although she was married in her youth, it's hard to imagine her as anyone's wife. Quite frankly, she is a bachelor; the *ette* suffix is simply too frivolous for a woman like Vail.

We went inside, my father insisting on carrying the heaviest of my things, and I was delighted to find that Vail had turned the heat way up in anticipation of our arrival—I could barely unzip my jacket, my fingers had become so stiff. Her little Jack Russell terrier leapt up to greet us, bouncing on the wood floor like a living tennis ball, and Vail began to show us the food items she had bought for dinner. Since she was not the cooking sort, this consisted of a deli container of clam chowder and a large vegetable assortment with a round well of ranch dressing in the middle. I volunteered to organize the heating of the soup, and while I did this, Vail complimented my cooking skills without a hint of sarcasm. I had to wonder about her definition of *cooking*, but I smiled and thanked her. She's had her own motorcycling streak, of course. When she lived in England for almost a decade, she owned several motorbikes and developed a fondness for driving on the left.

The evening passed quietly and Vail informed us that we would most likely miss each other in the morning, as she was going on a fox hunt very early. I nodded, as though foxhunting was something I did all the time, and then said good night and thank you for everything. The house was huge, and full of old newspapers and magazines, dead plants, and horse bridles and dog leashes over every doorknob, thrown over every chair.

My dad and I shared a room with two single beds, made up with sheets and blankets that had not been disturbed in years, perhaps even a decade. I slapped my pillow, and dust rose from it. My dad and I sat down on our respective beds and talked about how we might approach our first day on the road together. We had planned to pick up the Skyline Drive, and from there continue onto the Blue Ridge Parkway, which was to be the main feature of our trip together, but beyond that we hadn't really discussed much.

My dad looked up some directions to the northern end of the Skyline Drive on one of his gadgets, and eventually we turned out the light. In the morning, true to her word, Vail was already gone when we woke up, and so was the horse. We had a quick snack of blueberries and pistachios, and then carried our gear outside and strapped it onto our motorcycles. I could see I was going to have a little trouble backing up on the steep gravel driveway with all my stuff loaded up, but I didn't have to worry about it, because my dad was there. He gave me a hand, and what might have seemed like a dilemma to me only a day ago was no big deal.

After that, the first hour or two on the road was a little rocky. We got lost right off the bat, and the relief I had felt at relinquishing navigating duties quickly became exasperation at watching the person who was supposed to know where we were going get more and more turned around. The pros and cons of joining up with my father came to the surface immediately in those first few hours together, but eventually we found the Skyline Drive, and once we passed the little toll-booth entryway it didn't matter anymore. It was as though we had climbed to another level of the atmosphere. Clouds rolled across the road like tumbleweeds, and we rode right through them.

After a little while we pulled off onto one of the lookout shoulders and my dad lay down on the stone wall that edged the precipice and announced he was taking a nap. I am constantly amazed by his ability to fall asleep anywhere—in mid-sentence, for example, or on the edge of a steep drop. Some guys on Harleys pulled up and gave me a confused look. I shrugged at them and they moved on after a moment. When I started getting bored I took a picture of him with my cell phone, keys set on top of his chest like the bouquet at a funeral, hands folded across his abdomen, and sent it to my mom. She responded with raucous laughter, text message-style. After fifteen minutes or so he sat up with a sleepy gurgle and pronounced himself refreshed and ready to go. Sometimes hanging out with my father is a little bit like spending time with a cartoon character.

We continued on, stopping occasionally at the lookouts to check in with each other, to appreciate the rippling mountains stretched out before us, and to breathe the clear Appalachian air. As we continued I decided that the Skyline Drive was, without a doubt, the most beautiful road I had ever ridden on. The altitude, combined with the total seclusion, made it seem like another layer of civilization, something between the earth and the sky but part of neither. The road itself was so smooth, so well cared for, it was like riding on nothing at all. At the end of the 105-mile-long Skyline we crossed directly onto the Blue Ridge Parkway, which was just as spectacular, if not more so. We planned to traverse all 469 miles of it, from Virginia all the way down to the Smokies, at a leisurely pace. We had no deadlines, no place we needed to be. All my plans had led me here, to these mountains, and it was anyone's guess what lay for me beyond them.

As we rode, I realized that I had entered a part of the country that was totally unfamiliar to me—I had visited Vail once in Virginia, but the miles between her home in Boyce and my parents' home in New Smyrna were all brand-new to me. I get a jolt of inspiration from going where I've never gone before; I think covering new territory sparks dormant corners of the brain. With every new place comes a wider vision of the world—a more complete view and a better understanding of myself in relation to my surroundings.

I'd felt the same way five years earlier when my plane from Bangkok touched down in Australia. A new continent, a new hemisphere, a whole new way of looking at the seasons, at what north and south meant to me. When I landed, I knew I was there to stay—I hadn't been able to say the same throughout any of my travels, that next step had always been a question mark, but there, in Australia, I found new friends, a new family, and a new home waiting for me. Occupying such a radically different quadrant of the globe turned my inner compass on its head, and while riding along the Blue Ridge Parkway was not nearly so extreme or discombobulating, I couldn't help but react. It was a trip that widened my experience of the United States, contextualized it, and with that came a reevaluation of what *this* country, my home country, was all about.

THE GLOBAL EQUIVALENT of this reevaluation was somewhat more jarring, and hung in a different frame of reference. As I made a home for myself in Australia, met Thom's family and friends, and explored an unfamiliar city within an unfamiliar country, I began to lose track of where I had begun. In hindsight, I think that was the point. My origins as an American dimmed, and the stronger my Aussie life got, the fainter everything else became. I only wanted to blend in, to belong somewhere. In Ireland I had tried so hard to assimilate, to become one of them—contriving accents and drinking like it was a contest and going along with all the weird slang, even when I didn't understand it. By the time I ended up in Australia, I wasn't trying to hide anymore, I'd just forgotten where I'd begun, and the collage of sayings and customs and habits that I had picked up throughout my travels in Europe and Asia had melted into one fragmented identity.

I applied for a de facto spouse visa that was based entirely on my relationship with Thom. It necessitated combining our bank accounts, doing endless paperwork, spending a bunch of money, and proving our love over the past year to a government official (letters, photos, interviews, et cetera). While we waited for the visa, Thom found work with an Australian on-line HR company, writing ad copy, and I worked illegally at a tiny dress shop, where I lasted barely a month. The woman who owned the shop was my personal nightmare, constantly belittling everything about me: my country, my accent, my clothes.

Eventually, I quit, and then came the months of unemployment while we waited for the visa. We lived on Thom's paychecks, and even though Thom said he was happy to support us, I was drenched in guilt over not being self-sufficient for the first time since I'd left Vermont, and so I threw myself into projects at home. I baked—scones, muffins, cookies, pies. I cooked—compiling a thick black notebook of recipes I'd tried and would try again, filled with my notes and pink stains where blobs of made-from-scratch tomato sauce had been wiped away. I nested, hanging curtains and arranging "art" (postcards and posters) on the walls. And I waited—I waited for Thom to come home, I waited for the visa to be approved, I waited for one day to end and another to begin. If I hadn't loved Thom so very much I would've been unhappy, but I did love him, and for a time it was enough.

The visa finally came through and I was able to get a legal

job. I found myself behind the reception desk of a boutique market research firm, with black lines drawn around my eyes and tight pencil skirts shortening my steps. At first I was just relieved to be working—to have somewhere to go every day, something to do. With another paycheck coming in, a substantial one at that, we began to save. The need to revisit my childhood home, to see my parents, had been growing inside me since Thailand, and so we began to put something aside each month.

In the meantime, I felt the crush of inner-city commuters for the first time, the thrill of a nine-to-five life that only someone who has never had a nine-to-five job before can feel, however brief. It was all very domestic and grown-up, which is what I wanted after feeling afloat for so long. The routine was exciting for a moment, then unbearably boring.

When I think of Australia now, it's tempting to try to pinpoint where things went wrong and what I could have done to change it, but ultimately I was both happy and lonely there, lost and content, trapped and free to do what I liked. The game of trying to understand my twenty-year-old subconscious is interesting but ultimately futile—I was mixed up, acclimating to someone else's life in a new country and just trying to figure it all out, piece by piece. Thom was my best friend through all of it, and even when I began to feel trapped in Melbourne, he always knew how to set me at ease. We were a team, and we conquered each other's problems together.

Our home in Armadale was cozy, our kitten had a fenced courtyard to stalk birds in, I got on well with his family. His parents were always sweet, his two younger sisters would come visit us often, and even his aunts and uncles made me feel at home. Everything seemed complete.

Thom was close to his family, but he was even closer to his boyhood friends. There was a whole crew of them who had grown up together in a little town a few hours outside Melbourne, and I learned to love them, too. They were good guys, and even though they were never mine, even though the moment I hurt Thom they all fell away, as the friends of an ex tend to do, they were one of my favorite parts of Australia. I loved drinking beer and watching football and hearing about the women they chased and sometimes caught. I loved how deeply connected they all were, how most had traveled the world, yet still returned to the same city, same friends, same shared memories. There was an undercurrent of permanence in their tightly knit group that I envied, the intrinsic knowledge that they would know each other forever.

Instead, Thom was my permanence—the rock around which I built my idea of the future. In each scenario that passed through my mind, Thom was at the center. Neither of us wanted to get married, but with the de facto visa, the joint bank account, the way we shared everything, we might as well have been. We talked about going back to school, him for his master's, me for my bachelor's; we talked about traveling more, teaching ESL again; we talked about getting out of Armadale, a stuffy, domesticated part of the city, and moving to Carlton or Fitzroy—neighborhoods where instead of bridal shops and antiques stores there were hip cafés and young people and secondhand shops. It never crossed my mind, not even for a second, that we would part ways so soon.

AFTER ABOUT A YEAR of diligent saving, we went to the United States for what was intended as a long, leisurely visit—a four-month, cross-country-and-back-again road trip. We touched down in California, where we bought a car and drove north, up the coast, through Oregon and into Washington, where I saw my brother for the first time in seven years—a visit that both terrified and encouraged me. It reminded me that I *had* a brother, and then it reminded me that I had *this* brother. Thom stood by, awkwardly taking photos, while Phineas and I rehashed pieces of our childhood. We stayed for almost a week, and when we left I was both relieved to go and heartbroken to leave my brother. Phin has always had this way of inspiring contradictory emotions in me. I promised to come back soon—he didn't offer to visit.

Thom and I continued, through Idaho and into Montana, down into Wyoming, across South Dakota, through Iowa, Illinois, and Indiana, to Michigan, where I saw Detroit, my father's hometown, for the first time. I think Detroit is where things began to fall apart with Thom. There was no tangible event; it was just a sense of disconnection, as though he were drifting away from me—or vice versa. As though whatever had kept us together was eroding. The baseball games and the fishing and the family barbecue and even the Fourth of July fireworks all seemed to carry us further and further away from each other, and by the time we left, and dipped up into Canada, there was a tiny shard of doubt rattling around inside my rib cage like a piece of broken glass, and the more I moved, the more it hurt me. I still couldn't name it, couldn't look head-on at the possibility that we might not stay together, but it was there. Thom had predicted, years before, that I would one day break his heart. I laughed when he told me that, couldn't imagine ever not wanting to be with him, but now I wonder if he knew something I didn't. He was twenty-three when we met; I was eighteen. He always worried that I'd met him too young, and maybe he was right.

We left Canada, and went back down through New York and finally into Vermont, where my parents were waiting in the driveway of the house I grew up in—the house they had just sold—where I hadn't set foot for three and a half years. Thom and I had a fight in the car, maybe half an hour before we arrived. I don't even recall what it was about, something stupid I'm sure, I just remember gripping the steering wheel until my knuckles bulged, and wishing that when I turned my head the passenger's seat would be suddenly, mysteriously, empty.

. . .

NEWTON'S THIRD LAW states that every force has an equal
and opposite counterforce. Every action therefore has a reaction: I lift a book, and the book presses back on my hand
with an equal force, in the opposite direction; I press on the
ground with my foot and the ground presses back with an
equal force, again, obviously, in the opposite direction. According to this third law, there is no such thing as a solitary
force—by nature, it must create a reaction. It doesn't matter
which event is the action and which the reaction, because
both forces act simultaneously and there is not one without
the other.

Traveling with another person, a father, a friend, a lover, is
an inevitable challenge. Everyday relationships are difficult as
it is, but take one on the road, toss in some variables like finding new places to sleep and eat, getting lost, and getting de-
layed, and things become twice as hard. There is always
something not to like, always something to clash over that
sends both personalities flying backward like two bulls after a
sharp, confrontational *crack*, and it's always different, depending on whom you're with. There was no way to know that my
relationship with Thom wouldn't survive that trip, particularly after we had traversed Ireland, India, Thailand, and Australia hand in hand; there was no way to know that I wouldn't
go back to Australia, or hold my little ginger cat, or see Thom's
family, or watch another footy game with the boys, or walk

through Carlton Gardens, as I had done every day on my way to work. I pushed my life with Thom away, and it pushed back—with equal, and opposite, force.

THE SECOND DAY riding with my father on the Parkway was freezing. Clouds clung to the mountains and the sun was nowhere to be seen. We stopped for lunch at a little gift shop where they sold sandwiches and coffee. My gloves were useless in those temperatures; they weren't made for motorcycling at all, were in fact carpenter's gloves, which I had bought some time ago and ended up using for gardening. My father took off his own thick, insulated gloves and gave them to me. "What about you?" I asked him, and he said he would be fine, that he had another pair for warmer weather that he would use. "But then *you'll* be cold," I protested.

"This is what fathers do," he said, and he gave me a pat on the head.

Later, he presented me with a little pin he had gotten from the gift shop that said *Enjoy the view—Watch the road—Blue Ridge Parkway* and had an engraved picture of a motorcyclist on it. He had bought himself one, too, and we both attached them to our jackets. He was so proud of those pins—he still is. When I visit, he always asks me if I still have it, and I always do.

My father and I had our fair share of collisions, but after being thrown backward from the impact, we always seemed to return to each other. At one point on the Parkway he slammed on his brakes to make a wrong turn, and I had to stop so suddenly I almost ate road going forty miles an hour. He didn't even notice, just sped up when he realized it wasn't the correct left. I was so shaken I shrieked at him when he finally parked a few minutes later, and started seriously considering parting ways with him, continuing on to Florida solo. I sat on a big, flat rock by myself and cried a few tears of relief, and surprise, and fear, because I had almost forgotten that shitty things could happen, even with my dad here, even, sometimes, because of him. He got a sandwich at the overpriced Park restaurant while I steamed away, perched on my rock, and when he finally came back and offered to share it with me, I accepted, and we continued on.

At night, after we turned out the light but before we fell asleep, we would lie in the dark and sometimes he would ask me if I remembered how he used to throw me in the air and then catch me, or if I remembered the two pet rabbits who had so many bunnies they wouldn't fit in the hutch and we had to set them loose, or if I remembered the brush piles he used to make in the meadow, that he would then pour gasoline on and light with firecrackers. Reminiscing about the things we used to do together when I was little has been one of his favorite activities ever since we stopped doing those things.

Sometimes I remembered, sometimes I didn't, but it was remarkable to me how clear it all was to him. He's always had a way with small children—his silly, larger-than-life sense of humor thrills them to the core, and he in turn is thrilled as well. I suspect I had grown up much faster than he would have liked, our connection fading as I became more serious and less childish. I began to practice math by balancing my parents' checkbooks, then I started balancing them for real. My mother would rely on my brain as her grocery list: before we left for the store she would recite five or ten or even fifteen items to me, and I would memorize them. I didn't have time for my father's games, I was busy trying to be the youngest adult who ever lived.

We spent a week traveling along the Parkway, and as we crossed into North Carolina the foliage became widespread. Where before it had been only a tree here, a hillside there, suddenly it was as though the whole world were smoldering. The valleys below us were luminous with changing leaves. Tulip trees and hickories turning golden yellow, sassafras becoming orange, oaks and red maples, all exploding with color, while in the high altitudes the shaggy conifers lined the road, steadfast green sentries.

By the time we made it to Asheville, we were ready to take a break from being on the road. We stayed with friends of my father's in Bat Cave and took an extra day to rest there before continuing on. Flipping through a local newspaper, I saw an article about chimney swifts, small birds that roost in the same chimney in downtown Asheville every year when they fly south. It struck me as exactly the kind of thing my dad would have taken me to see when I was little, so we went to see the swifts the night before we hit the road again. It was just after the sun had set that they arrived in droves, flooding the sky and creating a living whirlpool that funneled into the chimney. It went on even as the sky darkened, birds arriving from every direction and adding their beating wings to the melee, until slowly the birds dwindled and disappeared. The chimney looked vacant—no way to know that inside it was teeming with thousands upon thousands of little swifts.

It reminded me of my father taking me once to see a flock of geese resting on a pond. He unfolded the tailgate of his truck for me, boosted me up, and told me that the geese were on a long, long journey, and when they got to where they were going, it would be time for them to turn around and do it all again. This made sense to me at the time—I figured that if *I* could fly, then I would probably want to fly and fly and never stop also. I would stop to sleep of course, to rest on a lake for a night or to catch a fish, but then I would beat my wings against the water and keep right on flying.

The next day we left Bat Cave and finished the last stretch of the Blue Ridge Parkway. At the end of it, we found ourselves in the small town of Cherokee, tucked between the end of the Parkway and the beginning of the Great Smoky Mountains National Park. The last piece of the Parkway had taken us the better part of the day, and so we spent the night in Cherokee, home of the Eastern Band of Cherokee Indians. We stayed in a sweet little motel that had two rocking chairs set out in front of every room. My dad and I sat in ours for a while, looking out at the mountains that loomed over the glaring neon of the reservation. It was a motorcycle mecca on account of its proximity to the Parkway and all the gambling possibilities, and the sounds of backfiring exhausts and revved-up engines echoed late into the night. The dark blue sky was mottled with even darker blue clouds and the kudzu vines carpeted the power lines, dripping down the poles like curtains. We ate fudge and looked at our motorcycles, talking about how much farther we had left to go, and where we would stop along the way.

We had come to the terminus of the Blue Ridge Parkway, and it would be highway from there on out, all truck stops and fast-moving traffic. After the idyll of the Parkway, it would be an abrupt transition, I knew, and would elicit a far different reaction, but I was feeling the pull of Florida; the comforts of arrival were beginning to sharpen in my mind, and so we planned to take the quickest route available to us, along Interstate 26, heading down into South Carolina.

18.

Buoyancy

My father and I developed an affinity for Waffle Houses. They were everywhere, they were cheap, and goddamn if the food wasn't pretty good. A creature of habit, my dad would order the same thing every time. Three over-medium eggs, wheat toast, hash browns, and decaf coffee—I still know it by heart. In a Georgia Waffle House, the fry cook waved me over when I walked in—my dad was getting gas—and asked me, "How 'bout them socks?" It took me a few minutes of asking him to repeat himself to figure out what the hell he was talking about, but eventually I realized he'd seen my Mass plate and wanted to talk baseball. "Ohhh," I said, "Sox." I don't really follow baseball, but he kept on talking, about a game I hadn't seen and a few players I hadn't heard of.

I just nodded and slipped in a couple of space-filling remarks, happy to be engaging with someone other than my father for a moment, even if we were talking about something I knew nothing about.

Eventually, the topic moved from baseball to motorcycles and I perked up. Ah, I thought, here we go, this I can talk about. He asked me if we were headed down to the Daytona Biketoberfest, and I said that we were, in a manner of speaking. I explained that my dad lived near there, and that we had met up in Virginia to ride down together.

"Well, good for you," he said. "I've been seeing brand-new Harleys roll through here all week, but none from so far away as Massachusetts. And with a little girl riding it! I'll be. Most of these guys trailer their bikes and drive 'em down."

I dissected the compliment from that remark and threw away the rest. The thing about the trailered motorcycles was true—all through South Carolina and into Georgia we had been seeing hordes of beautiful, shiny bikes, but most of them were strapped to the back of a truck. Just then my dad walked in and we got a booth. A waitress strolled over and asked us if we wanted coffee.

"Don't mind him, sweetheart, he's the village idiot," she said, jerking her thumb toward the fry cook and chuckling at her own joke.

"Don't you listen to a *word* that woman says," the fry cook shouted over. "She's just sour 'cause she ain't done nothing interesting in twenty years."

. . .

THAT WOULD HAVE BEEN our second-to-last day on the road. A few days previously, I had gotten an e-mail from the man I met at the Rainbow Diner in Pennsylvania, and he'd sent me a quick note and the website address for the tree house hostel in Georgia he had told me about. It turned out it was on our way, just past Savannah, so we decided to spend the night there. From the hostel it was only a four- or five-hour ride to New Smyrna, so it would be our last stop.

In terms of highway riding, we had only just managed to find a compromise. I thought my father went too slow, he thought I went too fast—we eventually agreed that 5 mph over the speed limit was acceptable to us both. I had also started making a point of writing down the day's route on little note cards before we began each morning and sticking them to my gas tank. As the trip wore on, I found I had less and less faith in my father's GPS system, so I slowly began to take over the navigation duties. My father graciously handed over this responsibility, and I started making note cards for him, too, just in case. I had lost him once or twice before, going too fast, of course.

After we left the diner I took the lead and found my way to Interstate 95. From there it would be a straight shot to the hostel, and then down to New Smyrna. As we sped along, I started to become excited about the conclusion of the trip. We were nearly there. At this point, I was tired of long days of riding, tired of living out of my duffel bag, tired of pressing on. Almost there, I kept telling myself, almost there.

It was right about then that the Magna stopped responding to the throttle and began to lose speed. I swooped over to the right lane, to be close to the shoulder should I need to pull over, and then tried again to accelerate with no response from the engine. The bike began to lose momentum more quickly after that, and so I put on my blinker and veered off into the breakdown lane. By the time I rolled to a stop, the engine had died completely so I hopped off the bike and started fiddling with things. I checked the gas line, that seemed okay, then I jiggled the spark plugs, thinking maybe they had come loose, but they seemed solid. My dad had pulled off behind me, and as he approached I took off my helmet and told him what had happened.

"Huh," he said, and a semi ripped past a few feet away. The bikes shuddered in its wake. I fiddled a little more, checking that all the exposed wires were secure, then I tried to restart the motorcycle. To my delight the engine turned over and almost caught—I tried again, this time with my hand on the throttle. I fed it a little gas and it roared back to life. I let it run for a minute and shrugged at my father.

"Well," I said, "I guess let's see what happens." He agreed, insisting that I go slow and stay in the right lane. We were less than an hour away from the hostel.

Things seemed to be going well, then fifteen minutes later

the same thing happened again, and again I was able to restart the motorcycle after messing with it for a few minutes. We kept going, but when it happened a third time we pulled off at the next exit and inquired about the nearest motorcycle mechanic at a gas station.

While we were stopped, my father wondered aloud if may be I had a bad tank of gasoline. This had happened to him recently, he said, and if that was the case then it was a relatively easy fix. There are a couple ways in which gas might go bad, but what he was talking about was water in the tank. Because water's density is higher than that of gas, the two substances separate and the water sinks to the bottom of the tank. If this happens, it essentially cuts off the gas supply and slowly starves the engine of the energy required to fire the pistons. The diagnosis would explain a lot, but we decided to get a mechanic's opinion anyway—after all, we'd already gotten the directions. Before we left, though, he poured a little gasoline dryer into my tank just in case, a substance that encourages the gasoline to absorb the water, which will then run through the engine as pure gas normally would. The problem lies in the separation of the two substances—they can be combined, but one will eventually separate from the other. Using a gas dryer delays this process and binds the two together.

It turned out that the shop we were directed to was a Harley dealership, and when I went inside and told the young, tattooed man behind the service desk that I was riding a

Honda and it was giving me trouble, he said the dealership only worked on Harleys. He did, however, direct me to another place that dealt with Japanese bikes a few miles away, so I located my dad, who had wandered off, and we got back on our motorcycles to go see what we could find.

WE WALKED INTO a huge empty showroom. One or two motorcycles, a four-wheeler, and a lone rack of accessories only made it seem emptier. I heard voices in the back, so despite the NO ADMITTANCE sign, I followed the sound and found a few mechanics hanging out in the service area. I told them my problem, and one of them stepped forward and told me to bring my bike around back. I did, and after about half an hour or so of troubleshooting, he admitted to having no idea what was wrong with it and then told me he had someplace to be.

"But," he said, "come back in a few hours and I'll keep working on it." I said okay, collected my dad, who had again wandered off and was chatting with someone on the phone, and in the interim we decided to take our chances with the Magna, head for the hostel, then come back after we ate something. By then it was getting late, we were both hungry, and I was truly annoyed at my motorcycle for taking me all this way only to fail me at the very last minute. It had been behaving pretty well since we'd used the gasoline dryer, but it's a scary thing to lose power on the freeway.

. . .

WHEN WE TURNED OFF onto the dirt driveway that would lead us to the hostel there were more problems. It had rained pretty heavily the night before, and so the road was a mess—huge puddles and lots of mud. I motioned for my dad to go first, and of course he zipped right through these obstacles. I followed, somewhat more hesitantly, until we came to the mother of all puddles. Maybe *lake* is a better word. It literally took up the entire road, and looked to be about two feet deep in the middle. My father stopped in front of it for a minute, then went ahead and gunned the engine, splashing right through the middle and up the other side.

Let me pause here and say that my father's motorcycle is much higher than mine, and is in fact a dual-sport bike, which means that it does pretty well in off-road situations. I knew right away that the puddle was a bad idea. My dad waited on the other side to see what I would do, and I just sat there looking at it, trying to decide if I could possibly skirt the edge—no—or maybe try to ride through where it was not quite so deep—again, no. As I contemplated my options, a little voice told me to stop being such a wuss, if he could do it I could do it, and so I ignored my well-informed doubts, aimed for the middle as my father had done, took a breath, and went for it.

It made me think of a dream I'd had a few weeks before, in which I was back on my trusty little Rebel, riding through the countryside, when suddenly I found myself approaching a pond that I had gone swimming in a lot when I was a kid. It was a beautiful, sunny day, and the pond sparkled like a big, murky-green gem. Zooming along, I began to bank left, so as to ride along the perimeter of the pond, only my motorcycle didn't respond. It kept going straight. I leaned hard and twisted my handlebars with all my might but to no avail—I was headed straight for the middle. In slow motion, I helplessly rode the length of the wooden dock that my father had built, and then plowed into the water, where my motorcycle sank beneath my furiously churning legs, lost forever to the depths.

In reality, I got halfway through the puddle when the mud reached up and grabbed my tires. I lost my momentum, the engine stalled, and the motorcycle went down. It was a lot like my dream, except that I didn't wake up in a sweaty sigh of relief. Instead of waking up, I got wet. I had enough presence of mind to flip the kill switch before I half swam, half climbed out, utterly drenched, covered in mud, and totally hysterical. As I sat on the bank and wailed, my father leapt into action. I don't know what I would have done if he hadn't been there. He plunged into the puddle, somehow started the Magna, and half rode, half dragged it up onto dry ground. The exhaust pipes were spraying muddy water everywhere, pretty much all my gear had been submerged, and the engine sounded like it was a drowning animal. I was a mess. My motorcycle was a mess. Everything I owned was a mess.

"Are you okay?" my dad asked me quietly.

It took me a few more minutes of despair before I could peel away my waterlogged jacket, scrape the mud off my helmet, and tell him that no, I was absolutely not okay. Miraculously, my motorcycle was. We pressed on.

STAYING IN A TREE HOUSE boosted my spirits somewhat. I changed out of my mud-soaked clothes, found a little cotton T-shirt dress that was somehow dry, and put that on. I hung a few things from the rafters, and regarded my boots with dismay. They were caked with mud, not only on the outside but inside as well. I put those under the bunk beds and tried not to think about them for the moment, then I went outside and explored a little. There were chickens everywhere, strutting around the main cropping of buildings, collecting bugs, and laying eggs wherever they felt the urge. Little wooden boardwalks zigzagged through the jungle, leading to other tree houses, to composting toilets and outdoor showers, to hiking trails and a garden and a labyrinth. It was a flower child's paradise, and my father, of course, was right at home.

After we had eaten and darkness had fallen, I took a flashlight and made my way to one of the outdoor showers. There was a moon that night, and as I stood in the hot, sulfur-scented water, washing the remnants of caked mud from my hair, I looked up at it and began to feel a little better.

I slept fitfully, and was eventually awoken just before dawn by two roosters crowing to each other from the branches of the live oaks. I heard my father get up and leave the tree house to commence his morning routine of jogging and meditating, and I drifted off again. By ten o'clock I had packed my soggy things and was ready to go. When he finally returned, he announced that he had found another way out—a road that was marked for service vehicles only, but that was paved and smooth. We got permission to use it, then we packed the motorcycles and rode out of the forest.

WE RESOLVED TO KEEP GOING and hope for the best. We were so close, after all. To be safe, after breakfast we stopped at a gas station and I bought another bottle of gasoline dryer. The whole motorcycle was covered in mud, and even though I wasn't really in the mood for this last leg of the trip, I couldn't help but admire how incredibly badass it looked. I wiped away a little of the grime from my license plate, but just enough to be legal, and then we got going, heading south— always south.

In physics, *buoyancy* is defined as an upward force that opposes the weight of an immersed object. Inside my gas tank, the two substances had separated, and the fuel was pushed up by the effects of buoyancy, whereas the water sank because of its comparative density. There is a clever trick for quantifying buoyancy: it is always equal to the weight of the displaced fluid. In its metaphysical use buoyancy is unquantifiable— it's the propensity for levity, the ability to recover, to float.

Weightlessness. But weight is intrinsic to buoyancy, they are cause and effect, and ultimately one defines the other. It's the weight that triggers the upward climb, because without the depths there would be no delicious gasp upon reaching the surface.

Soon enough we crossed the border into Florida and stopped at the welcome center, where they gave us small paper cups of freshly squeezed orange juice. The Magna had been running smoothly the entire way, and it seemed that my father had been right all along about the bad gasoline. It was a beautiful, clear day, and I began to see more palm trees with each passing mile. We stopped once more for gas and calculated we were a little more than an hour away. Jacksonville, with its hellish traffic, was behind us, and the rest was cake.

19.

Falling Bodies

We arrived in New Smyrna Beach tired but happy. My mother was in her garden out front, pulling weeds and listening for the sound of our engines. As we got off the motorcycles, she came toward us, waving her arms and smiling. I gave her a hug, and she smelled like sunscreen and fresh dirt and gardenias, as she always does in the summertime. After my dad and I had unloaded our gear and washed away the dust of our travels, we all sat down and had dinner together.

We ate early, and when we were done my dad came over and patted my head on his way into the kitchen. He decided to take the Magna for a spin around the neighborhood, because he still hadn't tried it out yet, and while he was gone, my mother and I sat together in her garden, propped up in lawn chairs. She pointed out her newest plantings: honeysuckle vines and firebush for the butterflies, her little citrus grove, with its fat green grapefruits hanging low, clusters of kumquats and huge Meyer lemons. The blue glass bottles she had hung from the branches of a live oak twirled and bobbed in the breeze, and the bamboo stalks quivered. Perfectly white clouds, like scoops of whipped cream, sped across the sky, and a feral cat darted into the yard, saw us, then slipped back out into the street. In the distance, I heard the familiar rumble of the Magna's engine, and my father came into view.

When the mosquitoes came out I went inside to unpack and put in a load of laundry. I threw everything—including the duffel bag itself—into the washing machine and added detergent. My father came in and reported that my tire pressure had been way too low, that I had practically been riding on sand for days and I was lucky not to be a smear on the highway. Of course, I hadn't noticed—didn't even remember when I'd last checked my tire pressure. I was just relieved to *be* somewhere, instead of always being on my way. After the past few weeks on the motorcycle, I was ready to pause for a beat. I hosed down the Magna until it sparkled and a little stream of mud ran down the driveway and into the street, then I threw the keys in a drawer and forgot about them for a while.

The next few months I stayed in Florida. In October I found an abandoned kitten in a torrential rainstorm, barely a week or two old, lying on her back in a pile of woodchips, and named her Maybe. I read, lay in the sun, went fishing with my dad, stayed up late watching television. Stillness settled, the pause stretched, and I began to worry about what came next. I wondered where I should go, whether I'd found what I was looking for, and what that was exactly.

I went to the beach in the evenings and mulled it over, just after the sun had set and the people with foldable chairs and kids and coolers had packed up and gone home. I would pick a direction and walk until it got dark, then I would turn around and walk back. I had begun to look for jobs in all sorts of places: Japan, Korea, Europe, New England, California. Location didn't matter, but it was time to move on, I could feel it. I made a list of the things I wanted and it was only three items long: I wanted to live alone, to keep the kitten I'd found, to not work in restaurants anymore.

In January I heard from an interesting job prospect back in Massachusetts, and I bought a one-way plane ticket for the interview, come what may. All of my things were there anyway. It felt odd to be going back to the place I'd just left, but I'd begun to recognize that the location of my feet mattered less than the substance in my head. All I needed was one thing to keep me curious and passionate and ambitious, and the rest would follow. For a while this had been motorcycles, but there's a whole world of fascination out there, an endless supply of mind-blowing possibilities. I had put the Magna on the market by then and I was ready for the launch—still unsure of where I was headed and what I would do when I got there, but aching for the challenge. A falling body is an object accelerating under the influence of gravity, and whether an object is thrown straight up, projected sideways, or released in mid-air, it will fall at the same rate. This rate is generally defined as 9.8 m/s^2 on earth, and while it can fluctuate slightly depending on geography, it is constant regardless of mass. Falling is such an uncertain, unreliable feeling. It helps to know that there are rules.

The motion of falling has captured me from the beginning. As a child, I was an outdoor gymnast, always climbing trees and doing tricks and jumping off things. On the property where I grew up, I had a balance beam, and I would rake the autumn leaves into a soft pile at the end for somersaulting into. And there was a rope swing, too, with a slim rectangle of wood for a seat and a single rope tied through the middle and knotted on the underside. The tree it was fastened to was an enormous maple, nestled into the cup of a steep hill. I would go down the hill to retrieve the swing, then run back up to one of two platforms my father had made at the top, one at the right and one at the left, and I would hold on to the rope with both hands and leap. Then, a delicious moment of suspension: the force of my legs pushing off from the ground would cease and the effects of gravity would take hold, pressing me back down toward the earth—only instead of dirt my feet would touch air, and the wooden rectangle would be under me, the rope in my hands and pressed against my cheek as I looked down more than thirty feet to the tall grass below.

That swing occupied me for years. Before I could manage it alone, my brother would swing with me. He would jump on first, and then I would wait at a more modest slope of the hill for him to swing back toward me so that I could hop onto his lap and we would swoop out over the meadow together. As soon as I was old enough, I mastered the simple art of leaping lightly onto the seat without him, then quickly moved on to more exciting challenges. I practiced mounting the wooden seat standing up, and holding the rope with one casual hand as I swept out over the meadow. I practiced jumping on backward—with my back to the hill and the heels of my feet at the edge of the platform. I practiced swinging upside down, then I practiced swinging upside down with one hand, then upside down with no hands at all, my legs wrapped tightly around the rope, my hair hanging down to kiss the grass.

Every time I perfected a new trick I would drag someone out to bear witness: my mother, my father, or Phin, and they would clap dutifully and I would name it something funny. The Brooks Double Twist. The Dalton Scrambler. The Rope-a-Dope. If I spent too long practicing, my hands would become chafed, and so my mother bought me a bag of white resin, like what baseball pitchers and serious gymnasts use. Tender calluses rose on my palms, soft and red at first, but they quickly became hard. I never felt more graceful, or more in control, than I did when I was upside down, thirty feet off the ground and counting, accelerating smoothly to reach an even loftier height. The motion of falling is familiar to me; I forget to think and I just feel.

In Florida, I thought of my next free fall. Leaping into the unknown, yet again, with no place to live and no job for certain and no real goal besides paying off my student loans, but there was a hint of possibility in the air, and the promise of things to come. As a teenager, I'd gone to Ireland trying to escape myself; in Australia, I finally did lose her. Returning to New England and falling for motorcycles was the beginning of realizing I wanted her back. Over the course of three years and four motorcycles, I learned a little more about who exactly I was looking for: a woman who has power and knows how to wield it, who knows when to hold fast and when to give way. A woman who is independent, resourceful, and strong enough to ask for help if she needs it.

I had taken leaps like this before—the only difference was the person doing the jumping. There was the landing to worry about, but whether one sticks the landing or gets a face full of dirt, it hardly matters. When I was practicing tricks on my childhood swing, the landing was always the easiest part. The trick was over, the risk either rewarded or wasted, and dismounting was simply a matter of waiting for the ground to arrive beneath my feet, then knowing when to let the swing slip away.

20.

Dark Matter

G rasping for some kind of spacer to put between myself and the world—a way to avoid it, or a way to control it—has always been my first and strongest instinct. I started by hiding my face in my mother's skirt; then, as I grew, I shielded myself with whatever was on hand: alcohol, drugs, traveling, other people, isolation.

Existing behind these barriers, finding ways to block out or alter an uncontrollable reality, made things easier, but it never made them better. On a motorcycle, I learned to let go of the vast uncertainty and focus instead on what is in front of me: the surface of the road and the curve of it, the vehicles in front and behind, the wind and the rain and the wildlife peeking out of the grass. There are times when I struggle to manage every last detail as it whips past me, to hold on to past and present and future simultaneously, but they're not mine to understand, or to control. I have to remind myself, again and again, that only this is mine: this moment, this heartbeat, this decision.

I'm just the navigator, riding through unfamiliar territory, in uncertain weather and unknowable traffic. There is only the thin shell of my helmet, the warmth of my own breath, and the road in front of me. The wind crashes against the sides of my head in waves, and the purr of the engine is like a mechanical *om*, shivering through me. The road rushes past and instead of struggling to possess it, I remember to exhale and feel the buzz of the pavement against my tires, the thrum of the open throttle beneath my palm. I remember that I don't own this road; I'm just using it.

WHEN I STARTED THINKING about the concept of matter, it seemed so simple, so universal, that I didn't consider much beyond the presence of matter and the absence of it, its composition and its dynamics—but more is unknown than known. Consider *dark matter*: the concept that some matter is visible—known and understood, cataloged and quantified—and that some matter simply *isn't*. It exists, but we can't see it or understand it, can't touch it, hear it, haven't the slightest clue what it's made of or how it moves. There is no direct evidence of dark matter, because its existence is currently impossible to verify, yet its effects are apparent in the behavior of visible matter throughout the universe.

When the theory of dark matter first arose, it was because of a discrepancy between cosmic mass calculations based first on a body's gravitational properties, and second on the same body's luminosity. The numbers didn't match: gravity was exerting a force far superior than the visible mass of the body and its surroundings would allow, so scientists began to consider the possibility of particles we couldn't see or detect that could be creating gravitational pull. Matter that neither absorbs light nor emits it, yet has enough mass to sway the movement of neighboring galaxies.

Now consider the accelerated expansion of the universe itself—not only does the universe contain more mass than we can account for, there is also some unknown energy at work, making it grow exponentially. If matter is the fabric of the universe, and energy the thread that binds it together, then what can we make of dark matter and dark energy? These ideas, abstract notions we can't see, can't prove, and can't explain, yet which make their presence known in some indirect way, aren't exactly new—I think some people call this God.

Ultimately, atoms, the regular matter that is the grass and the sun and every living thing on this planet, not to mention the planet itself, make up less than five percent of the universe. The remaining ninety-five percent is unknown, a mystery. It stands to reason, then, that what we *do* know is precious. Not only that, it's fleeting: a malleable, moldable, living thing. What I know now might need revising in one year, or ten, or twenty, but that doesn't make it any less important. It doesn't make it any less valuable. Even if what I know is nothing—that's important, too.

So this is what I think I know, right now: The universe is expanding; so am I. Of all the things to know, very few of them are known. Keep the truth close and keep it handy, it will almost certainly need reshaping. If in doubt, return to the foundation: examine the blocks, test their weight, their composition. Consider them as though for the first time. Take stock of what can be used, throw away the rest, and rebuild. Or, better yet—don't rebuild. Stack the elements and forgo the structure. Sleep under the stars instead, let the air move through the empty floor plan, and be awed by the infinite, unknowable dome overhead. Breathe. Expand. Forgive.

MY FATHER AND I took one last ride together before I sold the motorcycle and flew north. We rode out to Ormond Beach and turned onto the Loop, a scenic stretch of road that follows the coast and then doubles back through the wetlands. I smiled at the familiar sight of my father's motorcycle bobbing along in front of me and I breathed in the smell of hot, wet greenery and thick, black soil.

As we rode along the Loop, my father and I stopped at a small bridge that lifted to let a sailboat go through, and he turned off his engine while it passed. I kept mine running. I looked down at my instrument panel while we waited and thought of how much I would miss the rumble of this engine, and the curve of these handlebars, but I knew that there would be other motorcycles to love. After a moment, the sailboat passed, the bridge lowered, the gate lifted, and we moved on, over the river and back into the cool, dim marsh.

We took our time.

ACKNOWLEDGMENTS

This book is as much about family as it is about motorcycles, so I'd like to thank mine: thanks Mom, for your wisdom, unconditional support, and keen sense of beauty, and Dad, for your humor, super-sized heart, and intuition. Thank you both for holding me close as a child, letting me go as an adolescent, and taking me back with open arms when I was ready. Thanks also to my brother, for all the challenges and all the love—it's never been easy but it's always been worth it.

I want to thank my grandfather, Gordy Brooks, for the enigmatic advice and lovable wisecracks; Annie Brooks and Woody Rothe, for all their support; Denis Dalton, for reminding me how to have fun; and Vail Juhring, for the hospitality.

Thank you Jennifer Gates, my extraordinary agent, for taking this rough, flawed manuscript into your heart and helping it shine. Thanks also to everyone at Zachary Shuster Harmsworth for believing in me and in this story.

ACKNOWLEDGMENTS

Thank you, Ali Cardia, my wonderful editor, for giving this book a home at Riverhead and for your patience, insight, and encouragement—I am nothing short of blessed to have you in my corner. Deepest gratitude also to the multitude of Riverhead believers, helpers, and promoters.

I want to thank the group of Capstone 499, the very first readers of the very first chapters—in particular Jane Derderian, for taking the time to edit a rough draft in the midst of her own adventure, and also Shelby Kinney-Lang, for all the cheerleading.

There isn't room to thank everyone I'm grateful for, but there are a few friends I want to name who have been so incredibly supportive of this endeavor, from start to finish: thank you, Yana Tallon-Hicks, Malia Werle Gaffney, Isaac Pirie, Katie Koerten, Susan Kaplan, and especially Sally Clegg. Thank you, Ofurhe Igbinedion—you've been my anchor for the past thirteen years.

Thanks also to Amber Schaefer, Maisie Sibbison-Alves, Seth Capista, Nick Brown, Ian Tapscott, Tenaya Schnare, Ben Schnare, Anna Meyer, Nick Meyer, and so many others, for being a part of my story, whether on the page or off.

Thank you, Tenzin Rigdhen, for the motorcycle help and, Kannan Jagannathan, for the physics help. Thank you, Elizabeth McHale and Mira Bartok, for the suggestions in the early stages.

A very special thank-you to Matt Valliere—for everything.

Last but not least I want to acknowledge the teachers who guided me along the way: Bill Ackemann, who always wanted to know what I was reading; Joel Howes, who always wanted to see what I was writing; and especially John Hennessy, who believed in this book before I did—it would not exist without your encouragement. Thank you.